THIS BOOK BELONGS TO:

Published by Scholastic Australia in 2025.

Scholastic Australia Pty Limited
PO Box 579 Gosford NSW 2250
ABN 11 000 614 577
www.scholastic.com.au

Part of the Scholastic Group
Sydney · Auckland · New York · Toronto · London · Mexico City
New Delhi · Hong Kong · Buenos Aires · Puerto Rico

ISBN 978-1-76164-723-9

Printed in China.

Scholastic Australia's policy, in association with its printers, is to use papers that are renewable and made efficiently from wood grown in responsibly managed forests, so as to minimise its environmental footprint.

FACTS ABOUT FEELINGS

An Emotions Encyclopedia

Written by
Dana M. Winters, PhD
with Joëlle Murphy and Kristina Washington-Morris

Illustrated by
the Disney Storybook Art Team

Dear Parents and Guardians:

One of the most important things we can give a child is the opportunity to share what they are feeling. Encouraging your child to name and express what they are feeling not only brings the two of you closer but also has significant long-term benefits for your child's learning, behaviour and ability to form and sustain strong relationships with adults and peers.

This book gives adults and children an opportunity to share their feelings together. There are fifty emotions to explore. Each emotion is introduced with a story moment from one of your child's beloved Disney or Pixar movies. Each story moment includes related emotions to name and explore, examples of situations in which your child may feel these emotions, and thoughtful questions to guide the discussion. Keep in mind that there are no right or wrong answers to these questions.

As you read aloud, pause to talk about how a character might be feeling. Ask questions about why a character feels a certain way. How do the character's facial expression and body language convey that feeling? This will help your child put language and words to different emotions and provide important cues to determine how someone else might be feeling.

We hope this book supports an exploration of emotions as you and your child share your thoughts and feelings!

Contents

Introduction for Grown-Ups

Here are some things to consider when talking about feelings with your child.

Listen carefully and attentively.

Allow your child to speak fully and completely, and follow up with a question or two that can help them expand on what they are feeling.

Speak simply and honestly.

Use words that your child can easily understand, and be honest and open with your own feelings.

Share your own emotions.

When children see you demonstrate your own emotions in a healthy way or hear you talk about emotions with others, they will learn to do the same.

Include others.

Try to include family members and friends in these conversations when you can.

Build consistent opportunities to share.

Engaging in consistent conversations about feelings helps children view talking about emotions as something that is normal and necessary.

You don't have to be perfect.

Talking about emotions can be hard for both children and adults. It is okay to tell your child that you do not know and that you wonder about the same things.

We hope this book will serve as a starting point for conversations that support and celebrate your child's emotional growth and development.

Introduction for Kids

Riley's Emotions help guide her through the ups and downs of life. Which Emotions do you relate to the most? What are you feeling right now?

Being able to understand and share how we feel is an important skill. It helps our relationships with family, friends and the people around us.

There are so many feelings to explore. Let's get started!

Fear
is nervous and always on the lookout for danger. He does his best to keep Riley safe from all potential disasters.

Ennui
is slow and bored. She may seem lazy, but she can't be bothered to care too much.

Disgust
has expert judgment and is brutally honest. She makes sure Riley avoids all things smelly, uncool or gross.

Anger
can be impatient and impulsive. He can't help it. It's a tough job making sure Riley is treated fairly.

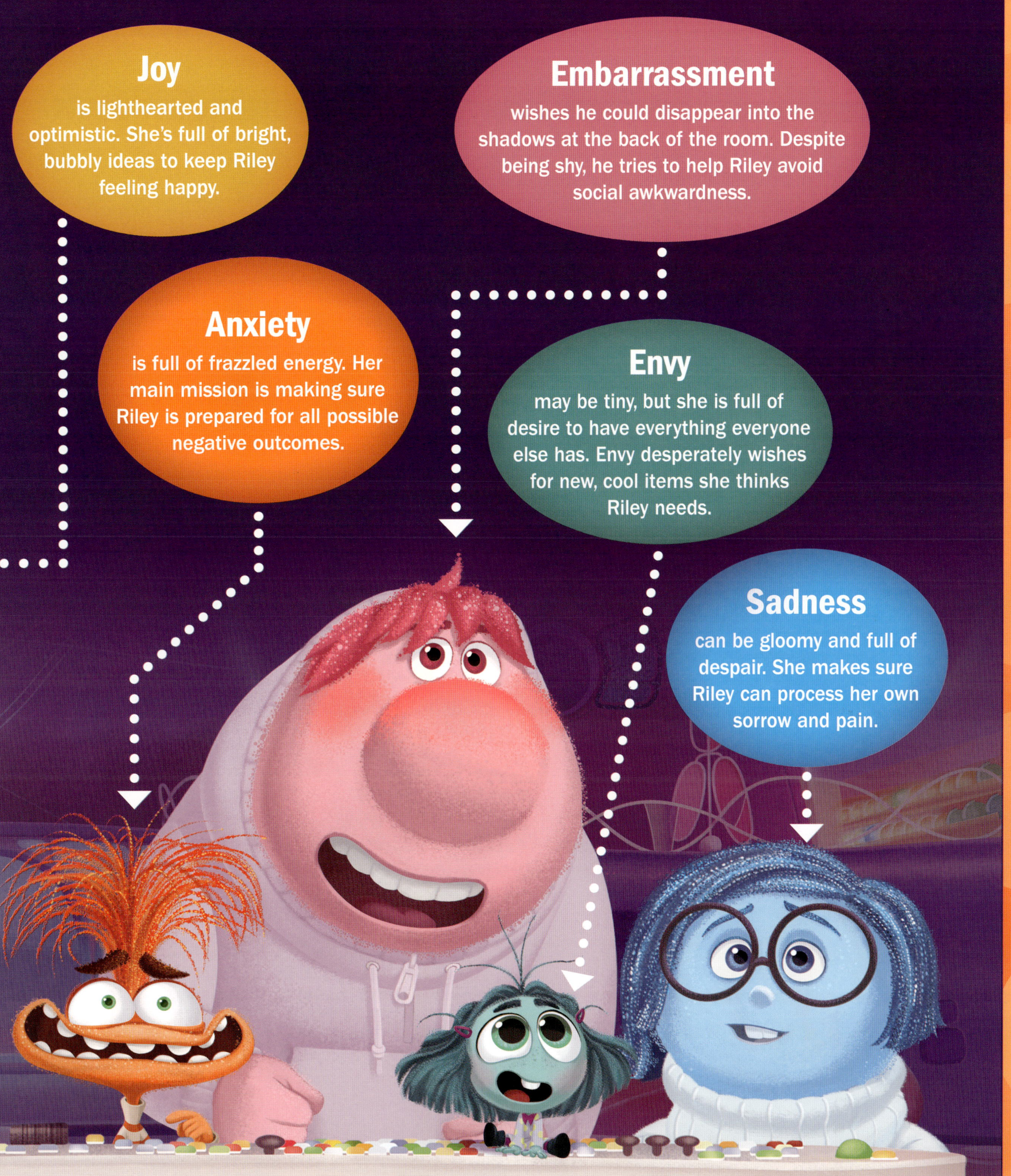
Joy
is lighthearted and optimistic. She's full of bright, bubbly ideas to keep Riley feeling happy.
Embarrassment
wishes he could disappear into the shadows at the back of the room. Despite being shy, he tries to help Riley avoid social awkwardness.
Anxiety
is full of frazzled energy. Her main mission is making sure Riley is prepared for all possible negative outcomes.
Envy
may be tiny, but she is full of desire to have everything everyone else has. Envy desperately wishes for new, cool items she thinks Riley needs.
Sadness
can be gloomy and full of despair. She makes sure Riley can process her own sorrow and pain.

Amazed

When Elsa heard a mysterious voice calling to her, she planned to discover who, or what, was reaching out. This led Elsa on a journey to the Enchanted Forest. Anna, Kristoff, Sven and Olaf joined Elsa on her quest north, into the unknown. After days of travelling, the group was **surprised** to find a vast wall of glittering mist. Elsa knew this was the Enchanted Forest and ran straight towards the glowing fog. The group felt **amazed** as they walked through the mist and emerged into the Enchanted Forest.

'This forest is beautiful,' Elsa said, in awe of the place she had only heard of in stories and songs.

Talking About It

People react to amazement in many ways. When Olaf first explored the Enchanted Forest, he gasped, giggled and even shrieked!

Have you ever been amazed when experiencing or seeing something new? How did you act when you were amazed?

What makes you feel
amazed
?
Something wonderful
A new experience
Something unusual
What's the Difference?
Amazed:
Filled with wonder by something or someone
Surprised:
Shocked by something unexpected

Annoyed

Lightning was lost and trying to find Mack. He headed down an exit ramp off the freeway. Suddenly, he heard a siren blaring and saw red lights flashing. A sheriff cruiser was after him! Lightning crashed through a fence, got tangled in fencing wire and roared through a sleepy little town, destroying its main street.

'You're in a heap of trouble,' Sheriff said when he caught up to Lightning. Lightning was forced to fix the road he tore up. He was **annoyed,** because no-one in town recognised him. He didn't feel like he deserved to be punished in this way. After all, he was a very famous race car, and famous race cars didn't fix roads!

He worked long into the afternoon, repaving the road in Radiator Springs. When he was finally finished, he was hot, tired and **aggravated!**

Talking About It

We can be annoyed with people or situations. Lightning was annoyed with the cars living in Radiator Springs and the task of fixing the road.

What is something that annoyed you recently, and what did you do about it?

What makes you feel
annoyed
?
Someone telling me what to do
Doing something I don't want to do
Not getting my way
What's the Difference?
Annoyed:
A little angry or irritated
Aggravated:
Angered or displeased by small problems

Anxious

Mike Wazowski had dreamt of working at Monsters, Inc. since he was in primary school. To achieve his dream, Mike needed to graduate from Monsters University, the school with the best Scaring Program!

To prove himself as a great Scarer, Mike joined the Oozma Kappa fraternity. The Oozma Kappas entered the yearly Scare Games. If the team won, Mike and his friends would surely be the best Scarers on campus! Some of the Oozma Kappas were **scared** to begin the Scare Games. Mike was especially **anxious,** because the Oozma Kappas needed to win to stay in the university's Scaring Program.

Talking About It

Winning the Scare Games was important to Mike and the other Oozma Kappas. They didn't know what to expect of the games, which made them feel anxious. We can feel anxious about big things and little things. What are some big or little things that give you anxious feelings?

When you are feeling anxious about something, what do you do? What helps you feel less anxious and afraid?

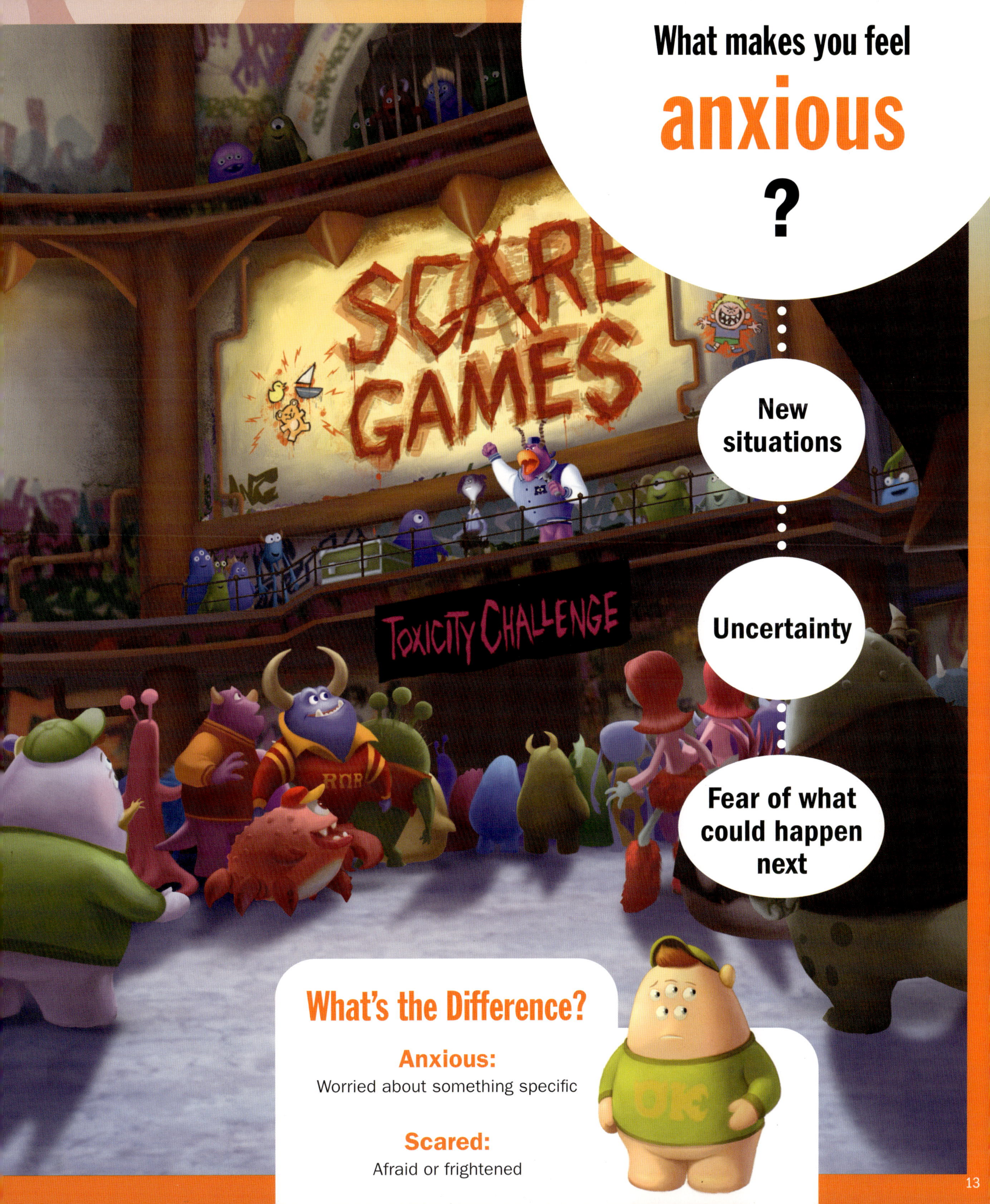

What makes you feel **anxious** ?

New situations

Uncertainty

Fear of what could happen next

What's the Difference?

Anxious:
Worried about something specific

Scared:
Afraid or frightened

Bitter

Scar, Mufasa's brother, did not attend Simba's presentation ceremony. He was unforgiving and **bitter** about no longer being next in line for the throne. Scar hatched a **vengeful** plan that involved killing Mufasa, blaming Simba and having Simba banished forever. Only then could Scar become king of the Pride Lands.

Talking About It

Scar wanted badly to be king. He felt bitter that Mufasa was king and that Simba would be next. When a situation doesn't go as we hoped, or we think life is unfair, we may feel angry or hurt. If we don't manage these emotions, they can make us feel bitter.

What are some ways you can express feeling angry, hurt or bitter without hurting someone else?

What makes you feel **bitter**?

Memories of being hurt or angry

Being treated unfairly

Someone having something I think I should have

What's the Difference?

Bitter:
Feeling hurt or upset for a long time

Vengeful:
Wanting to get back at someone out of anger

Bored

Joe was sure he could help 22 discover her Spark. The two hurried to the Hall of Everything. It held all that Earth had to offer.

Joe thought 22 might like baking. Baking didn't excite 22 at all. It wasn't her Spark. Next Joe thought 22 might like firefighting. It was not for her. He asked 22 if she wanted to be a portrait painter. Right away, 22 complained. 'Hands are hard.'

22 then tried being a scientist. 'Meh,' she said. She was **bored** and **tired** and didn't care about any of those professions.

An Olympic gymnast? President of the United States? An astronaut?

'Meh,' said 22. 'Earth is boring.'

Talking About It

We don't all like the same things. Joe liked to play the piano, but that might make others—like 22—feel bored.

What is something that makes you bored that other people like? What is something you like that might make other people bored?

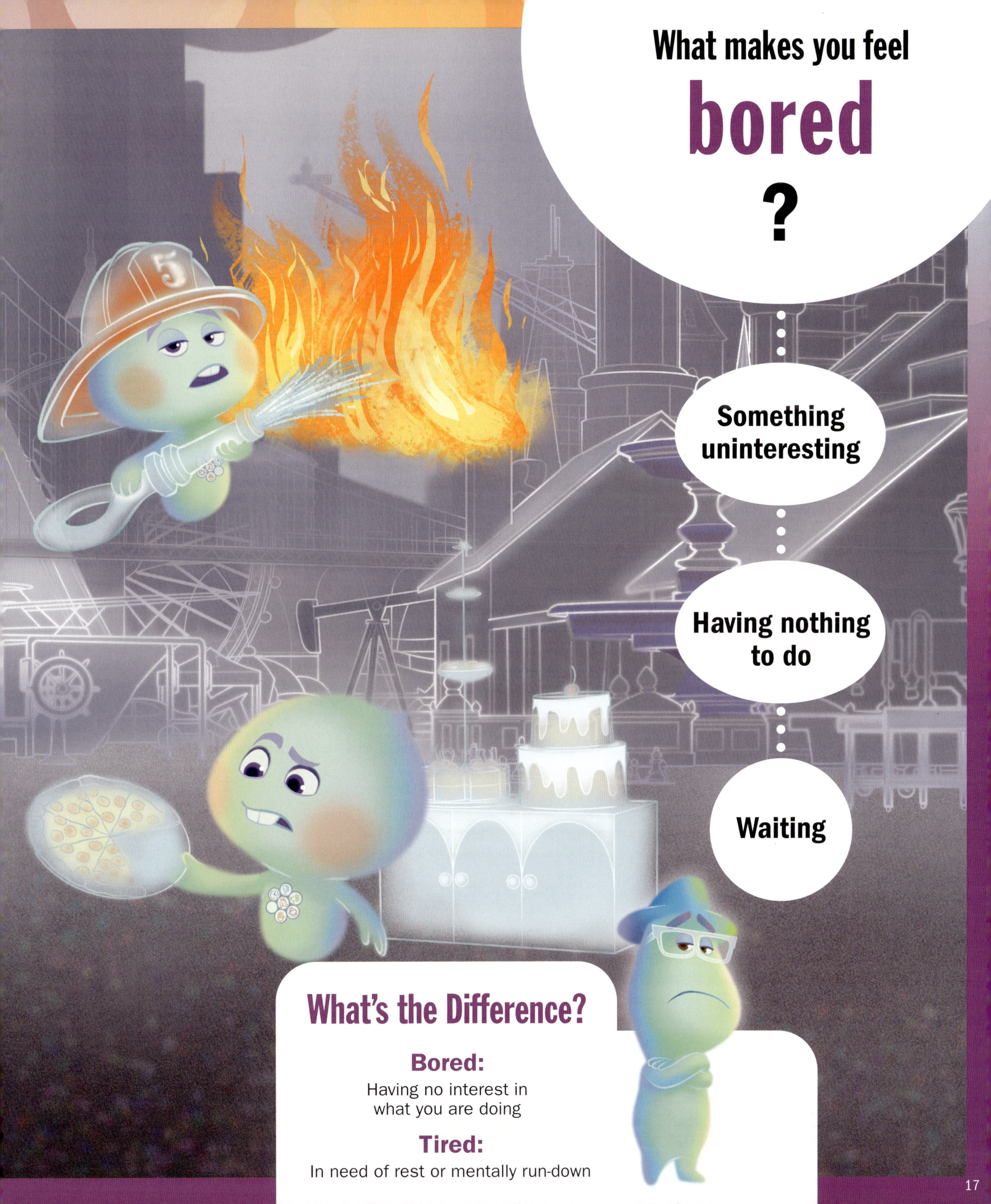

What makes you feel **bored** ?

Something uninteresting

Having nothing to do

Waiting

What's the Difference?

Bored:
Having no interest in what you are doing

Tired:
In need of rest or mentally run-down

Bothered

Guided by Gramma Tala and the ocean, Moana was on a quest to return the heart of Te Fiti. The first step of her quest was to get the demigod Maui to join her.

When Moana landed on Maui's island, she announced, 'I am Moana of Motunui and—'

But Maui kept interrupting her! Even after Moana explained her quest, Maui refused to help. Then he tried to take Moana's boat!

Moana was **bothered** and **agitated** by Maui's response. She had been counting on his help to return the heart of Te Fiti.

Talking About It

Moana thought Maui would agree to help her return the heart of Te Fiti. His interruptions and attitude bothered her.

Have you ever felt bothered by something a friend or family member has said?

What is something you can do when you feel bothered?

What makes you feel
bothered
?
Bad news
Not getting what I want
Not being able to figure something out
What's the Difference?
Bothered:
Concerned about something
Agitated:
Disturbed and upset

Brave

On the first day of school, Riley said goodbye to her parents and boldly and confidently went off to class. The day was going to be great! She was going to be **adventurous!** She didn't know anyone. She hadn't made any friends yet. At the beginning of class, Riley's teacher asked her about Minnesota. Riley was **brave** and talked about skating on the lake almost every weekend in winter.

Talking About It

Being brave can be hard, especially in new situations with new people. Riley found her bravery by talking about something she loved—skating on the lake. What is something you really love that would help you be brave in a new situation?

Have you ever been afraid to do something but found a way to be brave and do it? What helped you be brave? When do you feel the bravest?

What's the Difference?

Brave:
Having courage; ready to face something dangerous, scary or difficult

Adventurous:
Daring; not afraid to take risks

Calm

Raya and the last dragon, Sisu, planned to find the broken pieces of the Dragon Gem. Healing the Gem was the only way to defeat the Druun, a dark plague that roamed Kumandra.

Raya and Sisu travelled across the lands, meeting friends along the way who joined their mission. As they neared the final step of their journey, the friends stopped to eat and rest. Raya felt **calm** as she **relaxed** with her friends under the clear night sky. The peaceful moment helped prepare her mind and body to complete her mission and save Kumandra.

Talking About It

Friends like Tuk Tuk and Sisu helped Raya feel comfortable and calm. Are there people in your life who help you feel comfortable and calm?

Is there an activity, like reading, stargazing or eating a meal with your family, that brings you calm?

What makes you feel
calm
?
Being surrounded by supportive friends and family
Doing a quiet activity
Stretching or doing yoga
What's the Difference?
Calm:
Quiet and peaceful
Relaxed:
Being at rest and having a sense of ease

Caring

It was Carl's dream to visit Paradise Falls. With thousands of balloons and Russell's help, Carl flew his house within view of the breathtaking waterfall. While walking to the waterfall, Russell met an endangered bird.

'Don't be afraid,' Russell told the creature. 'I am a Wilderness Explorer, so I am a friend to all of nature.'

Russell convinced Carl and Dug to be **helpful** to the bird, which he named Kevin. Thanks to the **caring** trio, Kevin was reunited with her babies.

Talking About It

Carl and Russell became friends during their adventure. The friendship helped Carl show his caring feelings for Russell, Dug and Kevin. Later, Carl attended Russell's Wilderness Explorer ceremony. He even pinned on Russell's final badge!

Think of a friend, pet or family member you have caring feelings for. How do you express these feelings?

What makes you feel
caring
?
Thinking about others' needs
Listening to friends and family
Being kind to animals
What's the Difference?
Caring:
Feeling concern and kindness for others
Helpful:
Willing to give assistance or support to others

Comforted

While attending San Fransokyo Institute of Technology, Hiro's brother, Tadashi, invented an inflatable robot called Baymax. Tadashi explained what the large, soft robot could do: 'I programmed him with over ten thousand medical procedures and a caregiving interface that makes Baymax . . . Baymax.'

If Hiro scratched his arm, Baymax could apply bandages. If Hiro was sad, Baymax could give him a hug. Baymax's programming made sure his patients felt **relaxed** and **comforted.** Baymax would continue to care for patients until they felt better.

Talking About It

When Hiro felt sad and frustrated, Baymax suggested he reach out to a friend. Maybe talking with a caring person would help Hiro feel comforted.

Which people in your life make you feel comforted? How can you ask for help when you need to feel comforted?

What makes you feel comforted?

Being cared for by others

Having my feelings heard

Sharing a hug

What's the Difference?

Comforted:
Feeling calm and supported

Relaxed:
Being at rest and having a sense of ease

Confident

Riley and her team, the Foghorns, were playing in the hockey championship! As she skated down the ice, she could hear the crowd—and her parents—cheering. Riley loved hockey, and she especially enjoyed playing with her two best friends, Grace and Bree. Riley skated with skill and determination, but she accidentally tripped another player. Despite the mistake, she stayed **positive.**

The game was now tied, with only a few seconds to go. **Confident** in herself and her team, Riley called a special play. She sped towards the goal and, at the last second, passed the puck to Grace, who scored! The Foghorns won the championship!

Talking About It

Riley played hockey for years, practising hard to develop her skills. She also had a deep love for the sport. Have you ever worked hard to do something? Did it make you feel more confident? Has your enjoyment of something motivated you to practise more?

When you don't feel confident about something, what can you do? How do you build confidence in yourself?

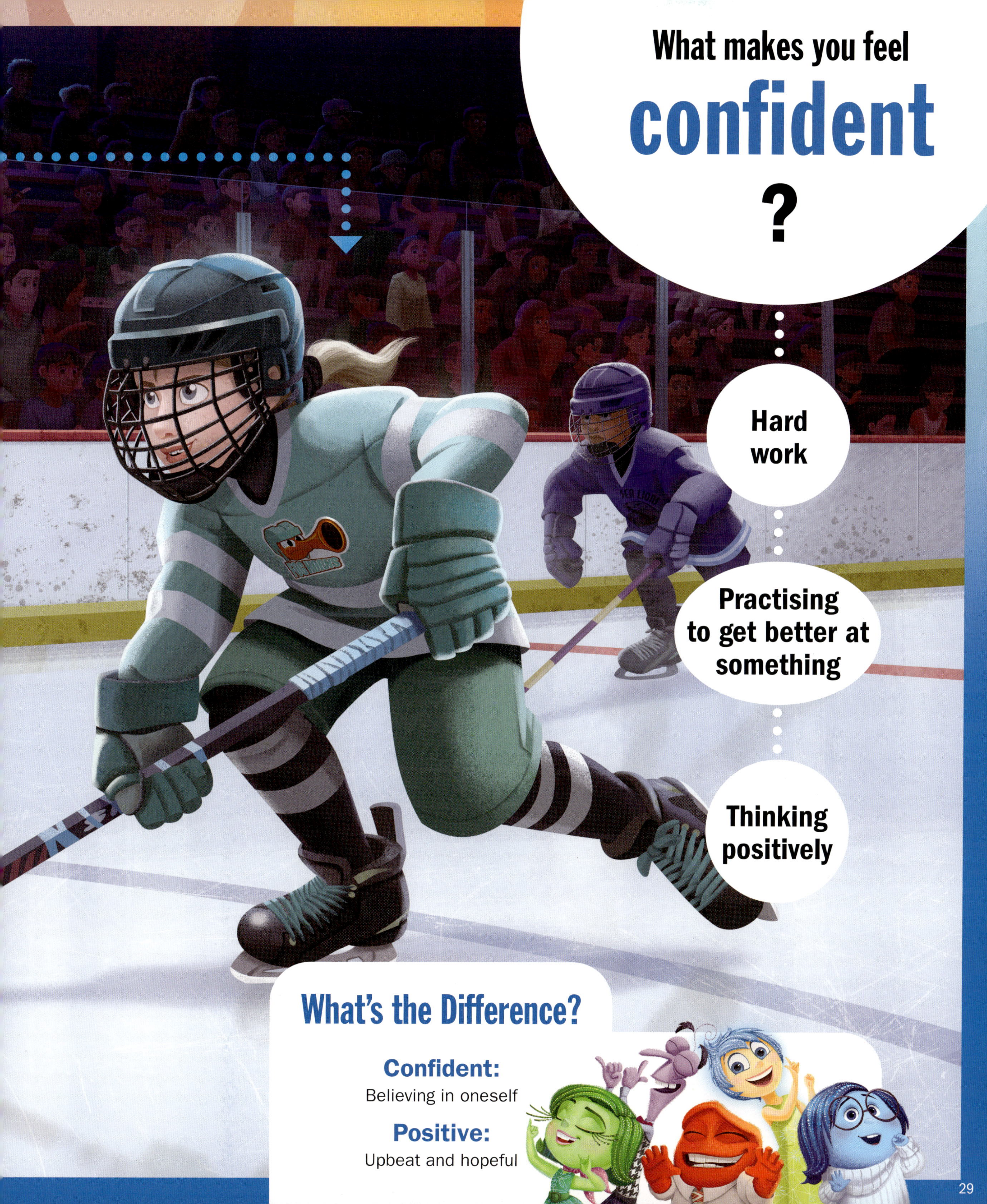
What makes you feel
confident
?
Hard work
Practising to get better at something
Thinking positively
What's the Difference?
Confident:
Believing in oneself
Positive:
Upbeat and hopeful

Confused

While enjoying a warm day in the park, Alice was distracted by a curiously panicked white rabbit. She chased after the rabbit and fell into Wonderland, a place of confusion and whimsy. After travelling on a beach and through a forest, Alice came upon a pink-and-white cottage. The White Rabbit ran out of the cottage. 'Why, Mary Ann!' he said to Alice. 'What are you doing here? I'm late! Go get my gloves!'

Alice wasn't sure why the White Rabbit called her Mary Ann, but she entered the cottage to find his gloves. Inside, Alice found a bowl of cookies. She munched on a cookie and felt herself growing. She was **alarmed** and **confused.** She kept growing and growing until she was bigger than the cottage itself!

Talking About It

Alice had many surprising encounters in Wonderland: the White Rabbit, who was always late; food and drink that made her grow or shrink; and even a Cheshire cat who answered her questions with confusing riddles.

When you are confused, what can you do to help ease the feeling?

What makes you feel
confused
?
Experiencing a new activity or event
Not understanding how I feel
Hearing lots of new information
What's the Difference?
Confused:
Not understanding, or feeling lost
Alarmed:
Feeling shock or sensing danger

Content

Baloo was Mowgli's new friend. He taught Mowgli about the bare necessities of life in the jungle.

He showed Mowgli how to find bananas, coconuts and other food. He showed him how to scratch his back on a tree too. The whole time, Baloo sang and danced.

Mowgli and Baloo played and splashed in the river and then floated downstream together, talking, laughing and singing. All was **calm** and peaceful. Mowgli was happy and **content.**

Talking About It

What are some things that make you feel content? When you feel that you are not content, what are things you can do to become happier and more peaceful?

When Mowgli and Baloo were floating down the river, they were both content and calm, enjoying each other's company. Are there people in your life who help you feel calm and content? What do you like to do with them?

What makes you feel
content
?
Relaxing with friends
Listening to music
Reading a book
What's the Difference?
Content:
Satisfied; peaceful and happy
Calm:
Quiet and peaceful

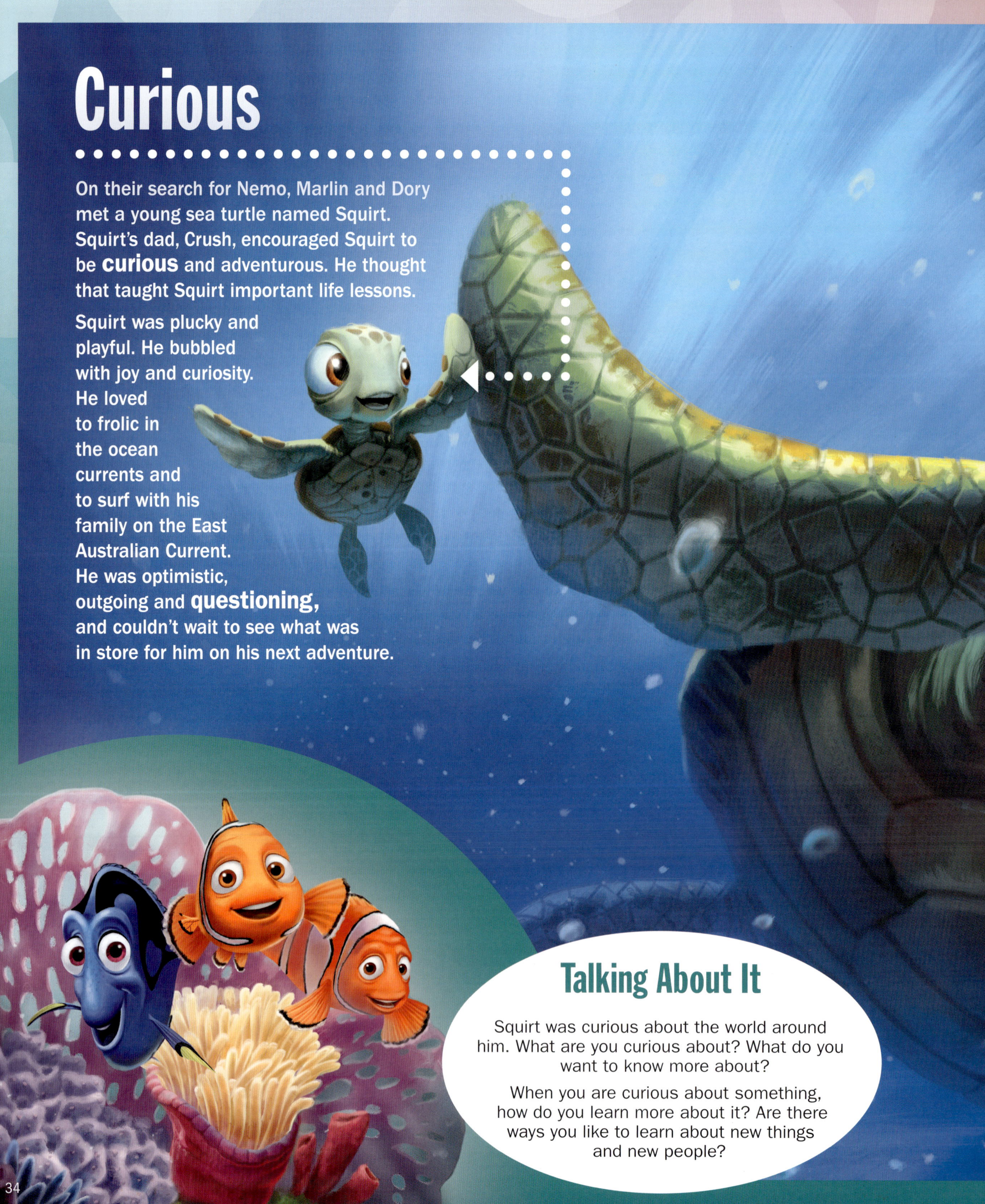

Curious

On their search for Nemo, Marlin and Dory met a young sea turtle named Squirt. Squirt's dad, Crush, encouraged Squirt to be **curious** and adventurous. He thought that taught Squirt important life lessons.

Squirt was plucky and playful. He bubbled with joy and curiosity. He loved to frolic in the ocean currents and to surf with his family on the East Australian Current. He was optimistic, outgoing and **questioning,** and couldn't wait to see what was in store for him on his next adventure.

Talking About It

Squirt was curious about the world around him. What are you curious about? What do you want to know more about?

When you are curious about something, how do you learn more about it? Are there ways you like to learn about new things and new people?

What makes you feel
curious
?
New topics
New people
Interesting things
What's the Difference?
Curious:
Excited to learn about or know something
Questioning:
Wondering and showing an interest in learning about something

Disappointed

Judy's lifelong dream finally came true! She graduated at the top of her class at the Police Academy. She reported to work for her first day as an officer with the ZPD, the Zootopia Police Department. Most of the ZPD officers were HUGE. But Judy didn't mind. Her nose quivered with excitement when Chief Bogo announced fourteen missing-mammal cases.

But Chief Bogo assigned Judy to parking duty instead. Judy felt **discouraged.** She worked so hard to be at the ZPD and be assigned her very first case. She was **disappointed** to learn her assignment was to ticket illegally parked vehicles.

Talking About It

Judy was excited to finally be a police officer, but she was disappointed when she didn't get the type of police work she wanted. Have you ever hoped for something that didn't work out? How did you feel when things didn't work out the way you wanted them to?

When you feel disappointed, are there things you can do to feel more hopeful and to keep working towards what you want? What are some times when you have felt disappointed and then felt better? What helped you feel better?

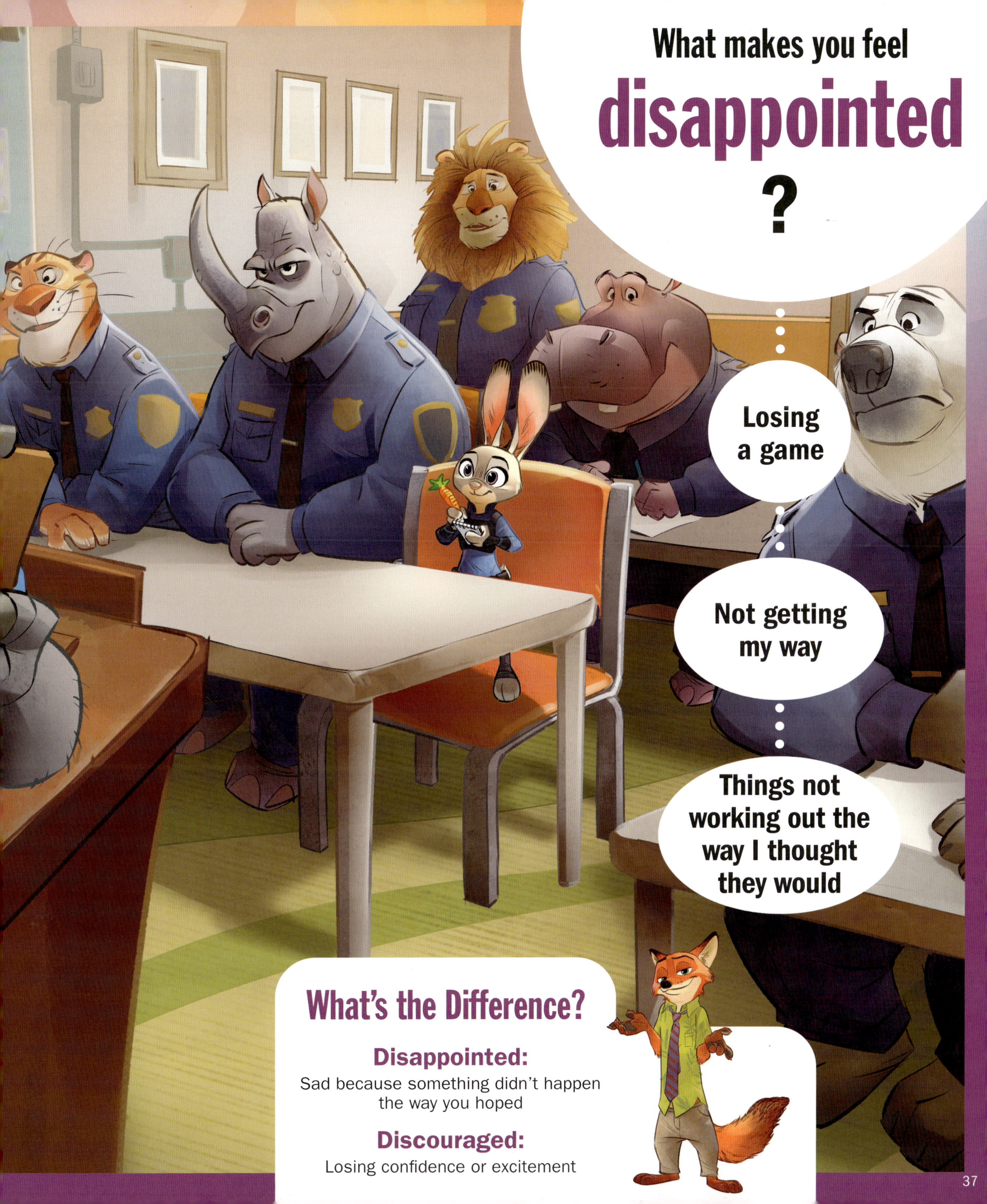
What makes you feel
disappointed
?
Losing a game
Not getting my way
Things not working out the way I thought they would
What's the Difference?
Disappointed:
Sad because something didn't happen the way you hoped
Discouraged:
Losing confidence or excitement

Disgusted

Luca and Alberto had a secret. They were sea monsters who transformed into humans on dry land. But if even a drop of water touched them while they were in their human forms, they would transform back into sea monsters.

Everyone in the town of Portorosso hated and feared sea monsters—no-one more so than the town bully, Ercole. During the biking portion of the race for the Portorosso Cup, Luca and Alberto got caught in the rain and transformed in front of everyone. With an **unhappy** Ercole after them, they sped through the course and crossed the finish line. They were declared the winners!

'Who cares if they won?' Ercole shouted, **disgusted.** 'Look at them!' He sneered. 'They're sea monsters!'

Talking About It

All kinds of things can make us feel disgusted—tastes, smells or the feel of something sticky. But feeling disgusted towards a person or a situation is different. When we feel disgusted by a person or a situation, we might have strong feelings of disapproval.

Ercole felt disgusted when he saw Luca and Alberto as sea monsters. How do you think that made Luca and Alberto feel? What could you do to help them feel better? What could you do to help Ercole feel better?

What makes you feel
disgusted
?
Someone or something I don't like
Something happening that I don't like
Someone or something that disappoints me
What's the Difference?
Disgusted:
Strongly disapproving
Unhappy:
Sad; not happy

Distracted

The evil sorcerer Jafar found Aladdin, a Diamond in the Rough—one deemed worthy enough to enter the Cave of Wonders. At the entrance to the Cave, Aladdin was warned to touch nothing but the lamp.

Aladdin's pet monkey, Abu, entered the Cave with Aladdin. There was treasure everywhere: huge piles of gold, gems and more. Abu saw a statue holding a glowing gem. He had to have the gem! Abu was so **distracted** by the beautiful gem that he was **indifferent** to the warning to touch nothing but the lamp.

'Abu! No!' Aladdin shouted from the top of the stairs. But it was too late.

'You have touched the forbidden treasure!' the Cave thundered.

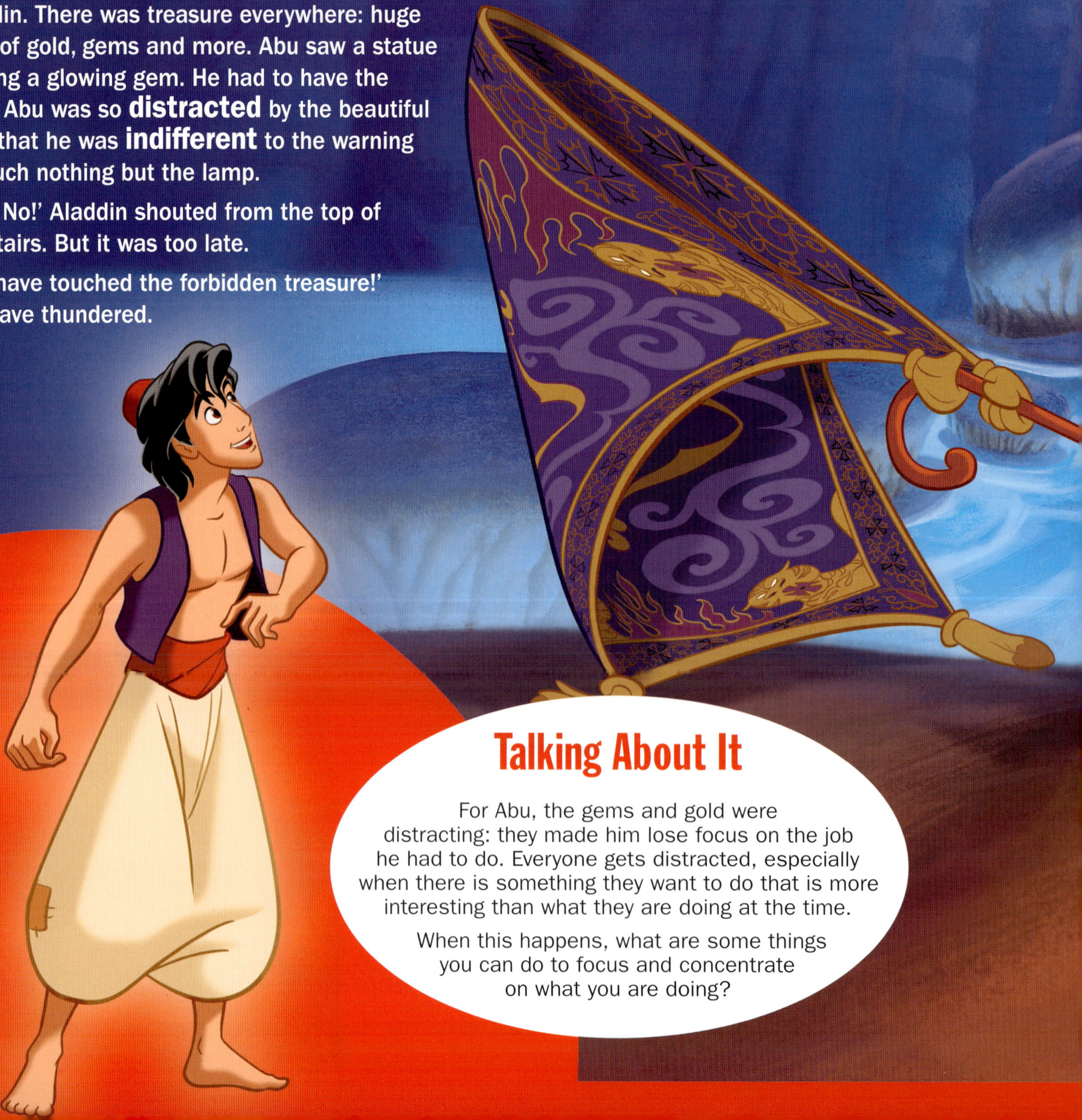

Talking About It

For Abu, the gems and gold were distracting: they made him lose focus on the job he had to do. Everyone gets distracted, especially when there is something they want to do that is more interesting than what they are doing at the time.

When this happens, what are some things you can do to focus and concentrate on what you are doing?

What makes you feel
distracted
?
Bright, flashy things
Too many thoughts in my head
Something more interesting than what I am doing
What's the Difference?
Distracted:
Having trouble focusing or concentrating
Indifferent:
Having no interest

Eager

Every morning, while the water heated for Lady Tremaine's tea, Cinderella fed the animals in the yard. The **restless** mice anticipated that moment every day and were **eager** to get their share.

One morning Lucifer, the cat, was blocking their way outside. They distracted him and made a dash for the yard, their tiny tummies longing for their food.

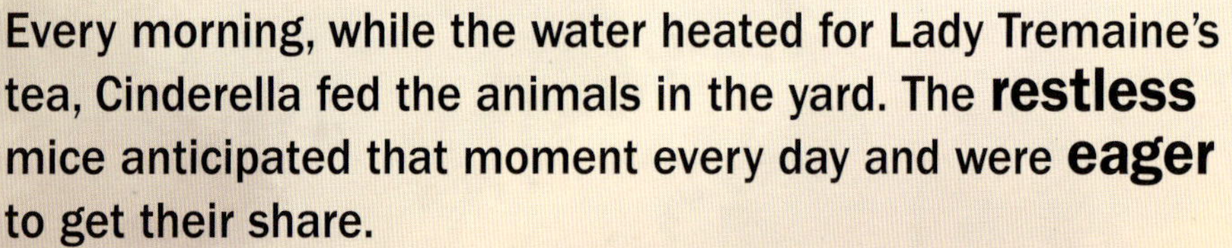

Cinderella had been waiting for the mice. 'Breakfast is served,' she said when they appeared. She scattered plump kernels of corn onto the ground for her hungry friends.

Talking About It

The animals were eager for food, but Cinderella was eager for something too—the royal ball! Is there an event you are eager about? How does it feel to be eager?

Sometimes when we are eager about something, we become impatient while waiting. What do you think the difference is between feeling eager and feeling impatient? How can you feel eager about something but stay patient while waiting for it to happen?

What makes you feel
eager
?
Something exciting
New experiences
Someone I enjoy being with
What's the Difference?
Eager:
Really wanting to do something
Restless:
Unable to relax

Embarrassed

Bob felt bad because he'd had Tony's memory erased. Violet liked Tony a lot, but now he didn't remember her at all! Bob tried to make it up to Violet by taking the family to the restaurant where Tony worked. Maybe the two teens would talk and resume their relationship.

Violet had no idea what her dad had planned. She took a long drink, looked up and was shocked to see Tony! Violet choked, and water spurted out of her nose. She felt so **embarrassed!** Bob tried to start a conversation, but Violet was too **agitated.** She would have given anything not to be there right at that moment.

Talking About It

Violet was so embarrassed by her dad trying to help, she chose to avoid Tony instead. If you are avoiding someone or something because you feel embarrassed, what might help the situation?

Embarrassment can come from feelings of fear, anger, nervousness or even disgust. How can you tell why you are embarrassed about someone or something?

What makes you feel **embarrassed**?

- Being shy or confused in public
- Making a mistake in front of others
- Speaking to big groups

What's the Difference?

Embarrassed:
Feeling stress about how others see you

Agitated:
Disturbed and upset

Excited

Buzz and Woody were running out of time! It was moving day, and Andy's favourite toys needed to catch up or they'd be left behind. Fortunately, Buzz had a rocket tied to his back. Woody lit the fuse, and the two toys blasted into the air.

Woody was **thrilled** and **excited** to be soaring in the sky. Buzz steered them through the car's sunroof and landed in the back seat, right next to Andy. Woody and Buzz made a great team. This was just the first of their many exciting adventures together.

Talking About It

Soaring across the sky was exciting, but being reunited with Andy was even better. Andy spent lots of time playing with his toys. He created stories and excitedly acted them out with Woody and Buzz.

What activities or events make you feel excited?

What makes you feel
excited
?
An upcoming party
Making plans to see friends
Getting to do something I love
What's the Difference?
Excited:
Feeling eager happiness
Thrilled:
Very pleased with a situation

Friendly

Sulley noticed that someone had left a door on the Scare Floor with its red light still on. Puzzled, Sulley peeked through the door.

Then something grabbed his tail. It was . . . a child!

Sulley thought kids were toxic. He tried to toss the little girl back into her bedroom. But the child would not leave. Giggling, she ran after Sulley as he fled into the locker room.

'Kitty!' she said happily. She was **friendly,** playful, **outgoing** and not at all afraid of Sulley. It was Sulley who was afraid of her!

Talking About It

Sulley was afraid of the child at first, until he realised she was friendly and wanted to play with him. Have you ever felt nervous around someone new and then found that they were friendly and wanted to be around you? Did that make you feel friendlier too?

When have you felt friendly towards new people or people you already knew?

What makes you feel **friendly**?

- Talking with someone
- Meeting new people
- Sharing something I like

What's the Difference?

Friendly:
Kind and interested in other people

Outgoing:
Confident around other people

Frustrated

The next-gen cars had arrived. Jackson Storm was a Next Gen. His smooth, aerodynamic form, modern build and high-tech training made him very successful at racing.

Lightning was **disappointed.** As Storm continued to win, Lightning continued to lose. And with each loss, Lightning felt more **frustrated.**

Talking About It

Lightning was frustrated because things weren't going the way he wanted them to, and that made him upset. What do you think Lightning could have done when he felt frustrated that he wasn't winning?

Have there been times when something has been hard for you and you have felt frustrated? What have you donc during these times so that you don't feel as frustrated?

What makes you feel **frustrated**?

Someone getting to do something I want to do

Something that is too hard

Not knowing what will happen next

What's the Difference?

Frustrated:
Bothered that things aren't going your way

Disappointed:
Sad because something didn't happen the way you hoped

Furious

Miguel had a secret: he loved music. But his abuelita made sure everyone followed the family rule: no music!

Strumming his homemade guitar in his hideout, Miguel played his heart out. The day came when he knew he had to tell his family about his dream. 'I'm gonna be a musician!' he announced.

Abuelita was **furious.** She grabbed his guitar and smashed it to pieces. Miguel was **dismayed.** How would he play in the talent show?

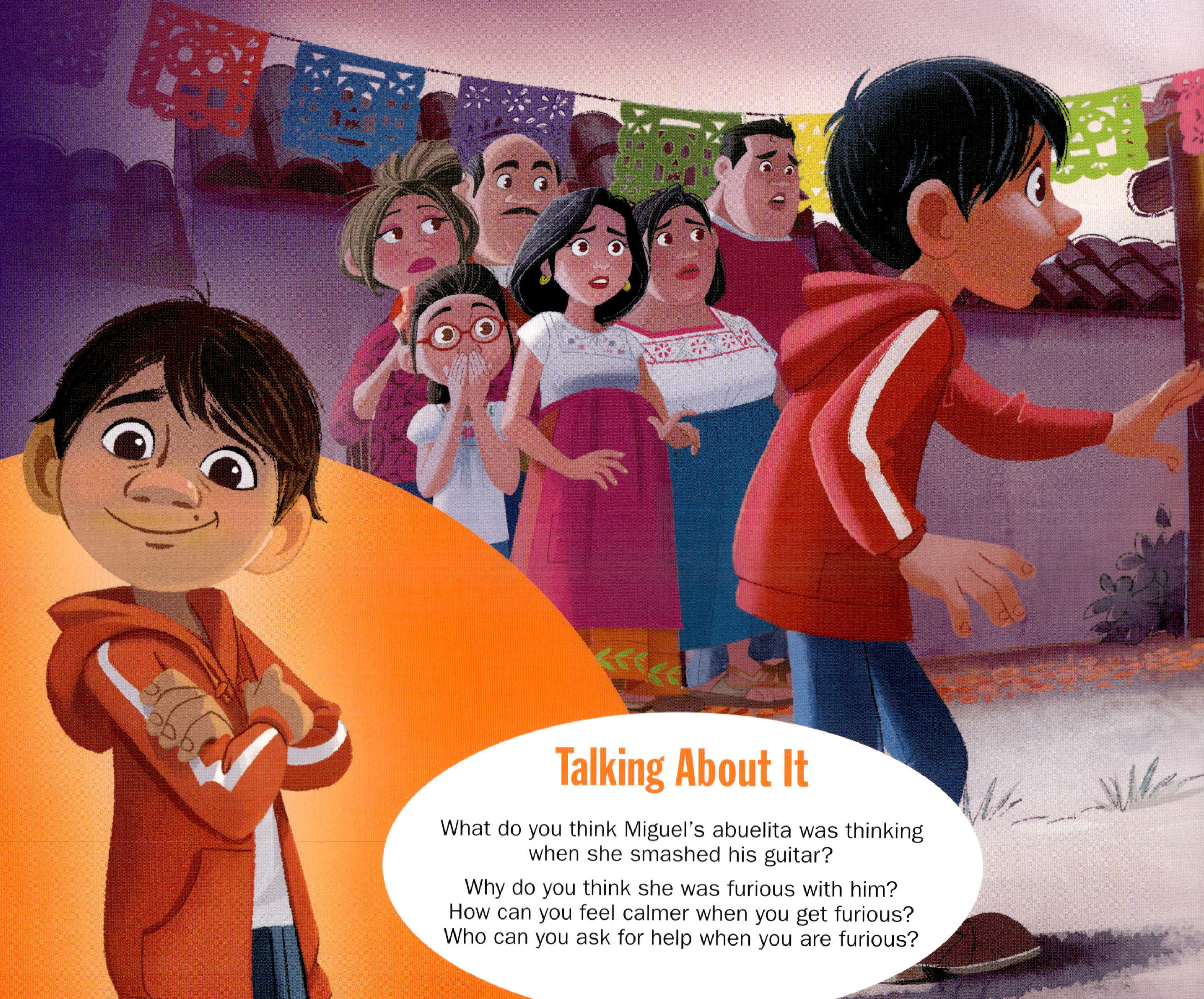

Talking About It

What do you think Miguel's abuelita was thinking when she smashed his guitar?

Why do you think she was furious with him?
How can you feel calmer when you get furious?
Who can you ask for help when you are furious?

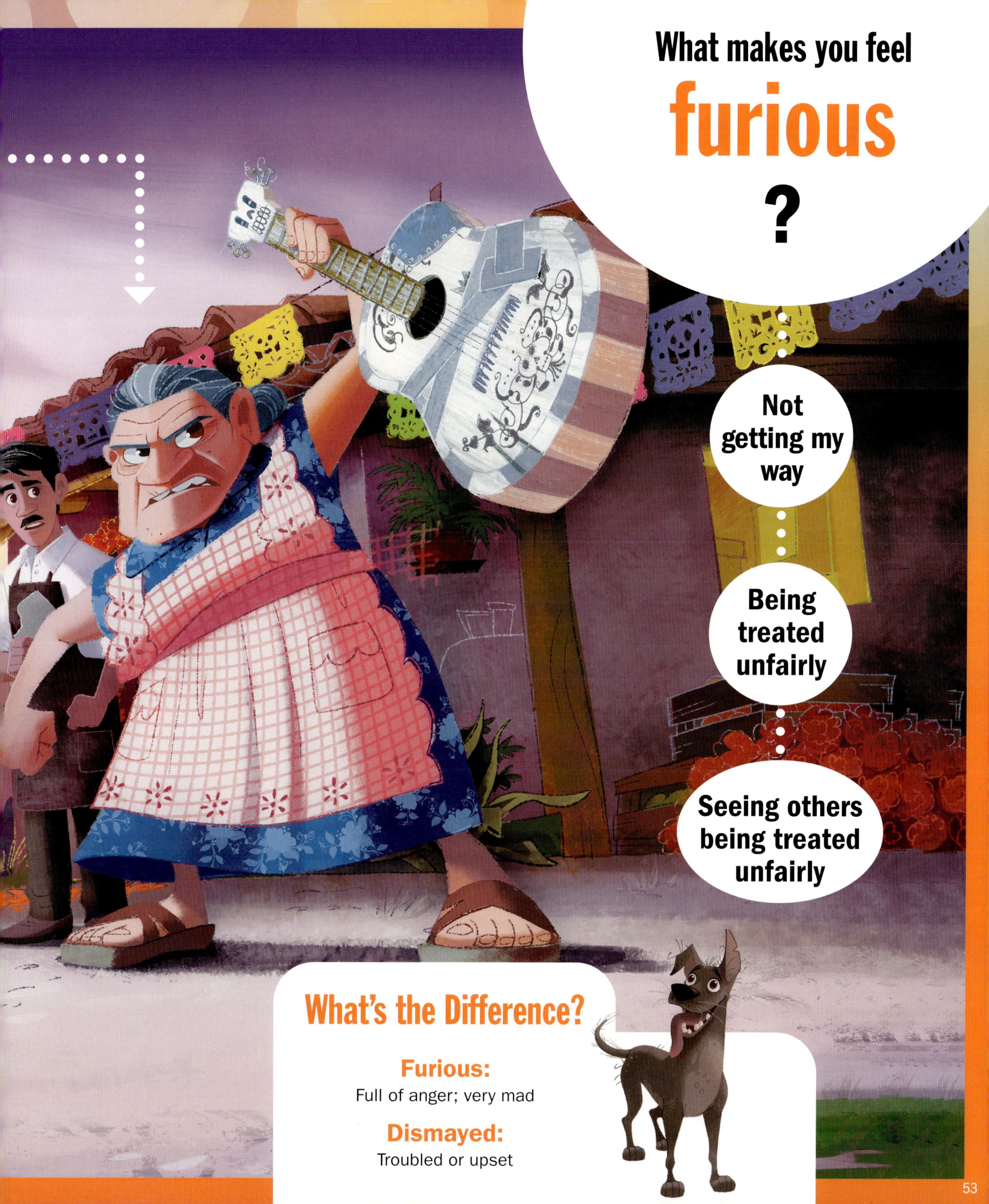
What makes you feel
furious
?
Not getting my way
Being treated unfairly
Seeing others being treated unfairly
What's the Difference?
Furious:
Full of anger; very mad
Dismayed:
Troubled or upset

Grumpy

Supers were now illegal. Helen was chosen to go on a mission to convince everyone that Supers were very much needed. She got a new Supersuit and a new jet-powered motorcycle—the Elasticycle. Bob would stay home and take care of the kids.

The first night Helen was away, she called home. Bob answered, and Helen nearly burst with excitement. 'I saved a runaway train! It was so great!' She recounted the whole story while Bob checked the news channels. He couldn't help feeling jealous as every station reported on Elastigirl's heroics. Suddenly **moody,** Bob became very, very **grumpy.** His eyebrows furrowed, his mouth hardened and his hand tightened around the phone.

Talking About It

When Helen was out enjoying a mission without him, Bob was jealous and in a bad mood. He was grumpy that Helen got to be the hero while he had to stay home.

When you are in a bad mood, what are some things you do to feel better? If you can tell that other people around you are grumpy, what can you do to help them feel better?

What makes you feel
grumpy
?
Not getting my way
Disagreeing with someone
Doing something I don't want to do
What's the Difference?
Grumpy:
In a bad mood
Moody:
Having sudden changes in mood, sometimes getting sad

Guilty

Despite Jiminy Cricket's warnings, Pinocchio made poor decisions and found himself locked in a cage. Fortunately, the Blue Fairy came to help. But she wanted to know why Pinocchio didn't go to school.

Pinocchio made up an excuse. As the lie fell from his mouth, his nose began to grow! 'Perhaps you haven't been telling the truth, Pinocchio,' the Blue Fairy said.

Pinocchio felt **guilty** and **ashamed** for lying. He promised to tell the truth from that moment on.

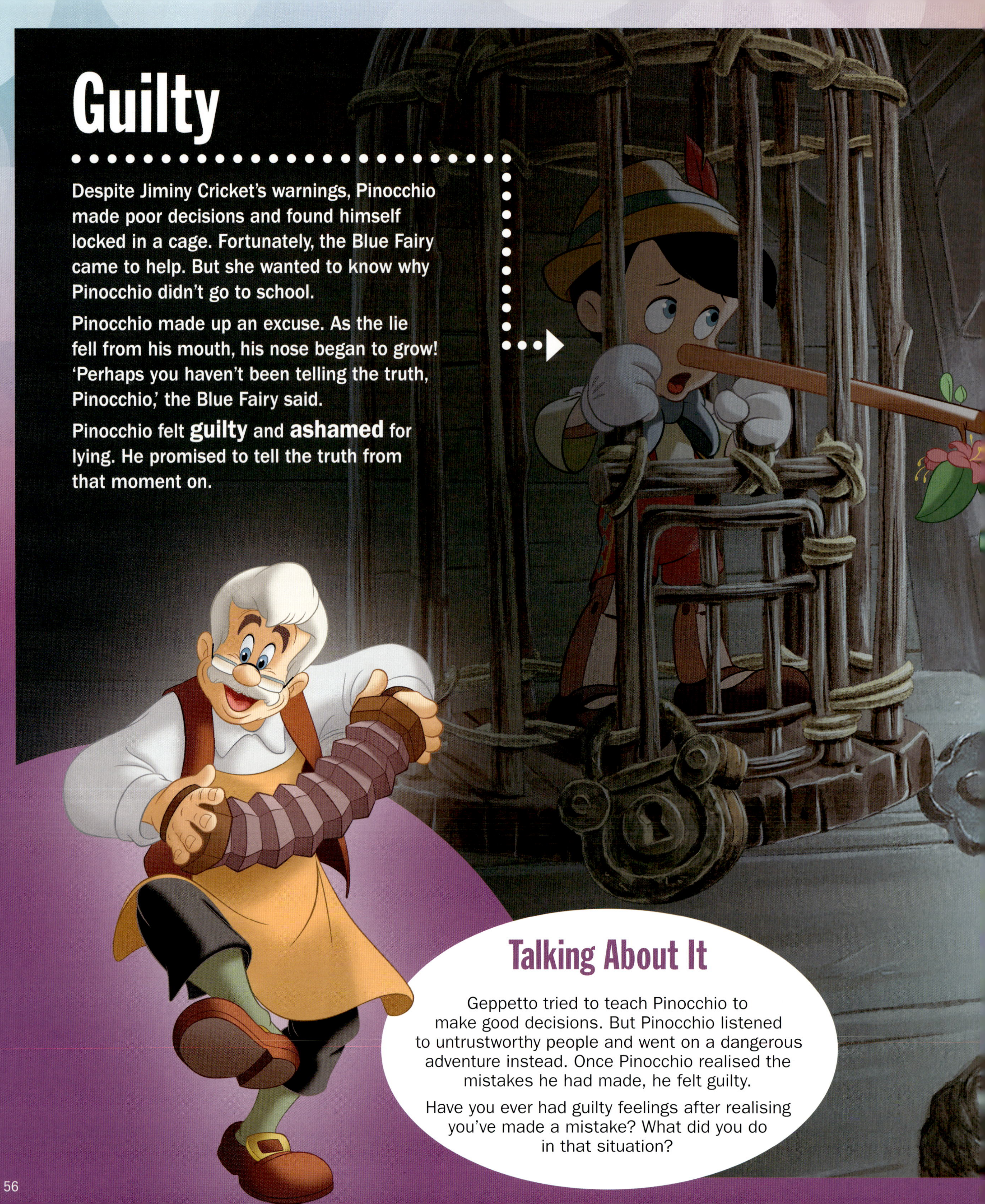

Talking About It

Geppetto tried to teach Pinocchio to make good decisions. But Pinocchio listened to untrustworthy people and went on a dangerous adventure instead. Once Pinocchio realised the mistakes he had made, he felt guilty.

Have you ever had guilty feelings after realising you've made a mistake? What did you do in that situation?

What makes you feel
guilty
?
Knowing I've done something wrong
Thinking I'm responsible for something that went wrong
Saying something that hurts someone's feelings
What's the Difference?
Guilty:
Feeling responsible for something that went wrong
Ashamed:
Deeply regretful about something you did

Happy

Rapunzel's dream to see the lanterns filling up the sky was hours away from coming true. She couldn't wait.

Elated, Rapunzel and Flynn joined hands and began to whirl around the square. They were carried away by the music and the dance, and they were **happy** being together.

Later Flynn led Rapunzel to a boat and rowed them to a spot with a perfect view of the kingdom.

As lanterns filled the sky, Rapunzel's heart soared with joy and happiness. Flynn handed Rapunzel her own lantern and helped her send it aloft.

Talking About It

Rapunzel had always dreamt of seeing the lanterns. When she finally got to see them, she was so happy. What is something you waited a long time to do and you felt happy when it finally happened?

What do you like to do when you are feeling happy? Do you like to share your happy feelings with others? How do you share your happy feelings?

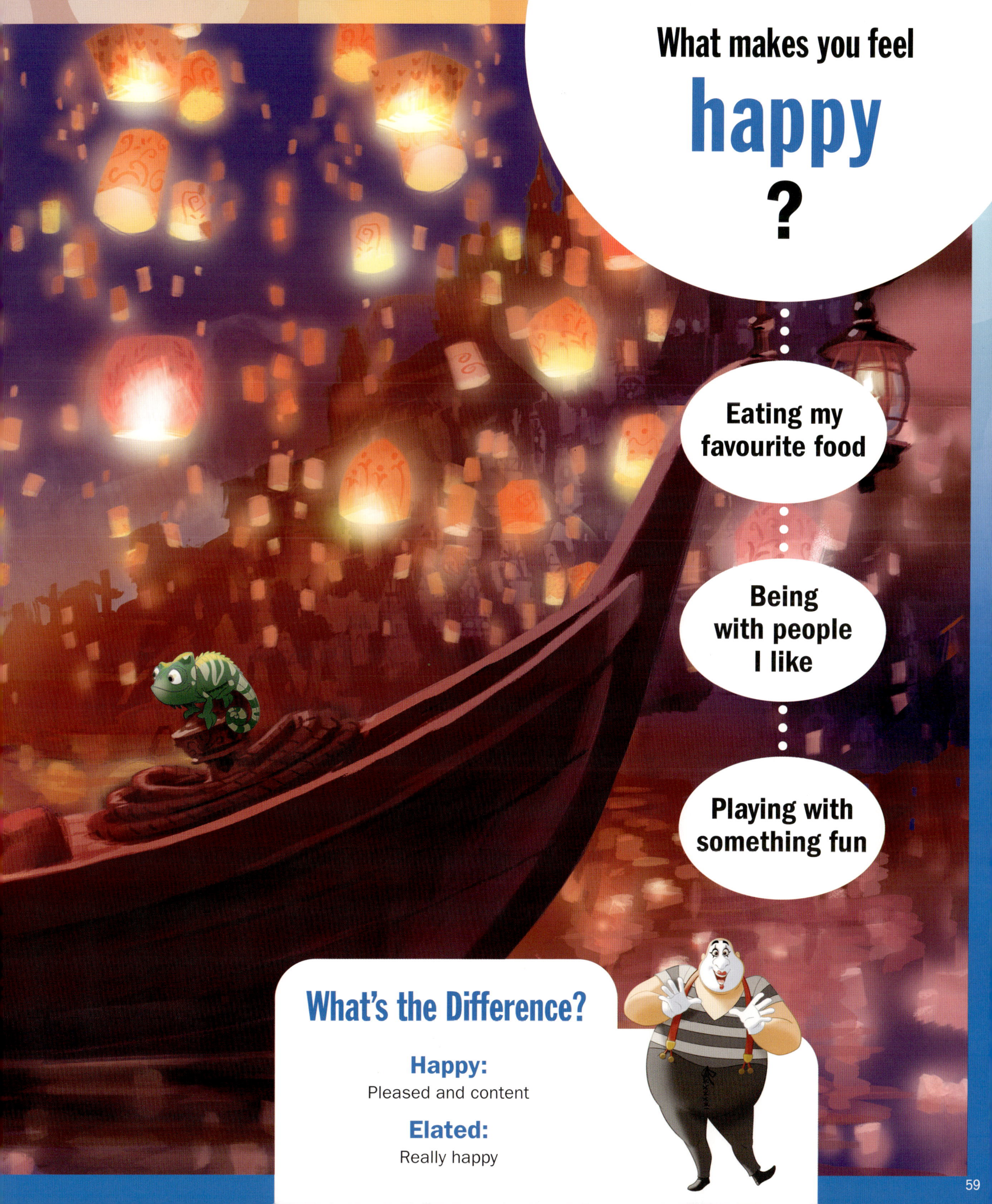
What makes you feel
happy
?
Eating my favourite food
Being with people I like
Playing with something fun
What's the Difference?
Happy:
Pleased and content
Elated:
Really happy

Hateful

King Stefan and the Queen did not invite the evil fairy Maleficent to celebrate the birth of their daughter, Aurora. Maleficent appeared, **hateful** and wicked. She had a gift to bestow on the princess. 'Before the sun sets on her sixteenth birthday,' Maleficent declared, an **unpleasant** grin sweeping across her face, 'she shall prick her finger on the spindle of a spinning wheel and die!'

Maleficent felt she did not get the respect she deserved. So she got revenge by cursing the child to death.

'Seize that creature!' King Stefan cried to the palace guards. But Maleficent just laughed. She raised her arms and disappeared in an eruption of green fire.

Talking About It

Maleficent was so filled with hatred that she cursed Aurora to get back at King Stefan and the Queen.

Have you ever been so angry with someone that you wanted to get back at them for what they did to you? How did you handle feeling like you hated someone else?

What makes you feel hateful?

Being left out

Wanting what someone else has

Someone saying mean things about me

What's the Difference?

Hateful:
Filled with hatred

Unpleasant:
Disagreeable;
filled with unhappiness

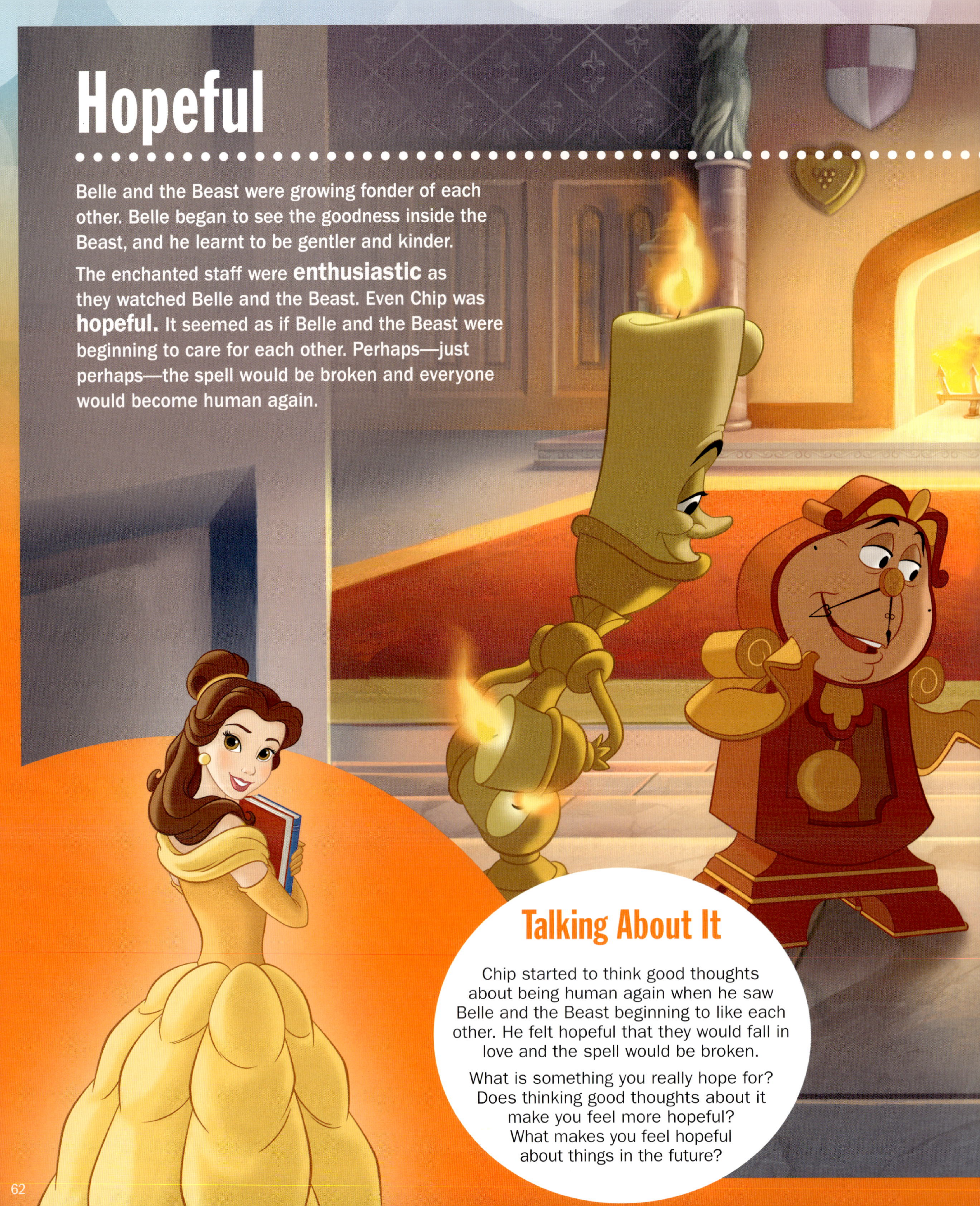

Hopeful

Belle and the Beast were growing fonder of each other. Belle began to see the goodness inside the Beast, and he learnt to be gentler and kinder.

The enchanted staff were **enthusiastic** as they watched Belle and the Beast. Even Chip was **hopeful.** It seemed as if Belle and the Beast were beginning to care for each other. Perhaps—just perhaps—the spell would be broken and everyone would become human again.

Talking About It

Chip started to think good thoughts about being human again when he saw Belle and the Beast beginning to like each other. He felt hopeful that they would fall in love and the spell would be broken.

What is something you really hope for? Does thinking good thoughts about it make you feel more hopeful? What makes you feel hopeful about things in the future?

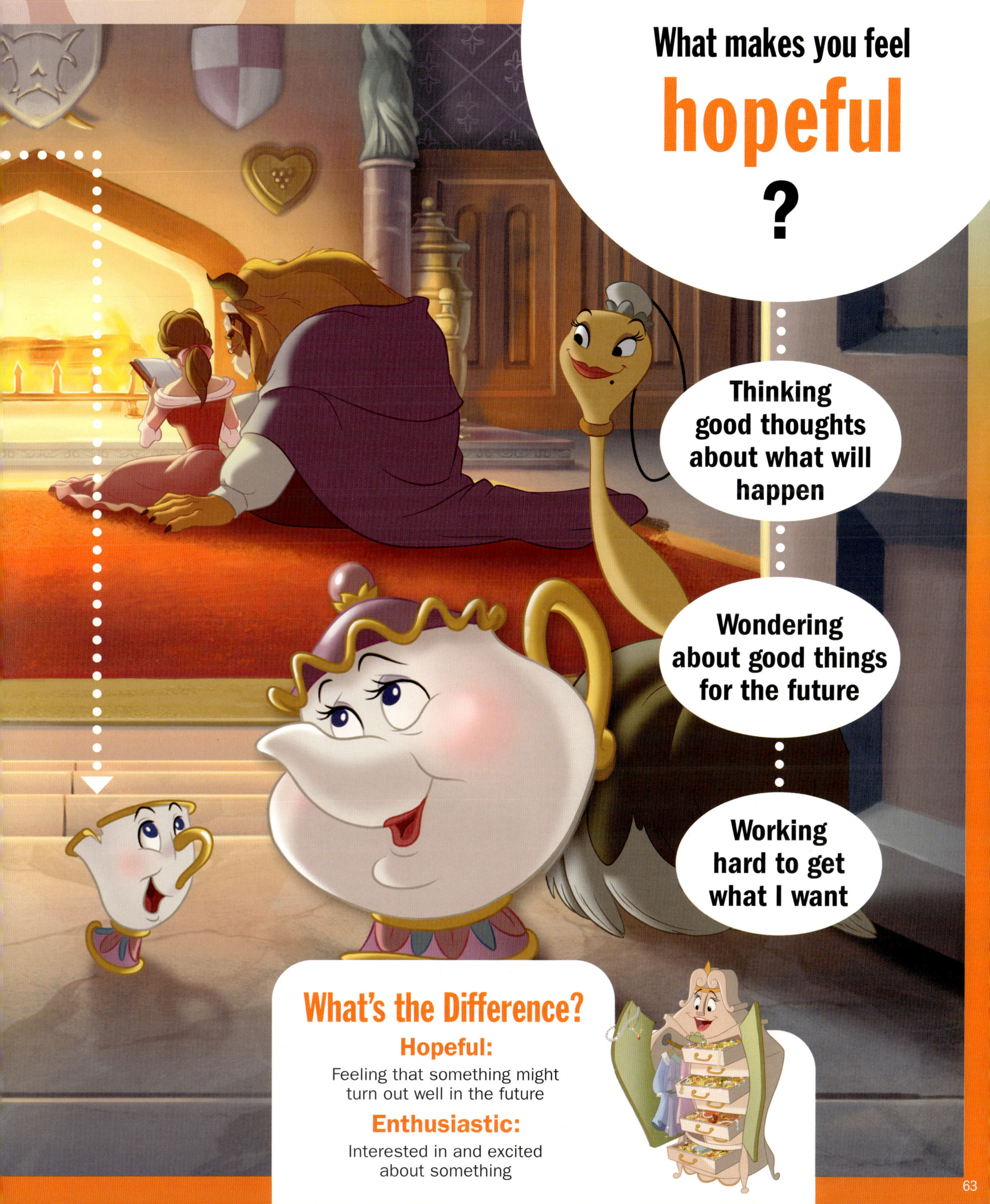
What makes you feel
hopeful
?
Thinking good thoughts about what will happen
Wondering about good things for the future
Working hard to get what I want
What's the Difference?
Hopeful:
Feeling that something might turn out well in the future
Enthusiastic:
Interested in and excited about something

Hurt

Meilin, Priya, Miriam and Abby dreamt of going to the 4*Town concert. 4*Town was their absolute favourite band. The four friends found creative ways to make money for their concert tickets. Mei posed for photos and attended a party as the Red Panda Girl, and the girls sold panda-themed merchandise. They couldn't wait to go to the concert!

When Mei's mum, Ming, learnt how the girls had been making money, she was upset. Ming accused Mei's friends of taking advantage of Mei and blamed them for her behaviour. Mei stayed quiet. She didn't defend her friends or admit that the "panda hustle" was actually her idea.

'Mei! Tell her,' pleaded Miriam. Priya, Miriam and Abby were **hurt** and **offended** that Mei didn't tell her mum the truth.

Talking About It

Mei hurt her friends' feelings when she didn't stand up for them. It took some time, and an apology from Mei, before her friends forgave her.

Have you ever hurt someone's feelings or had your feelings hurt by someone? What helped the situation?

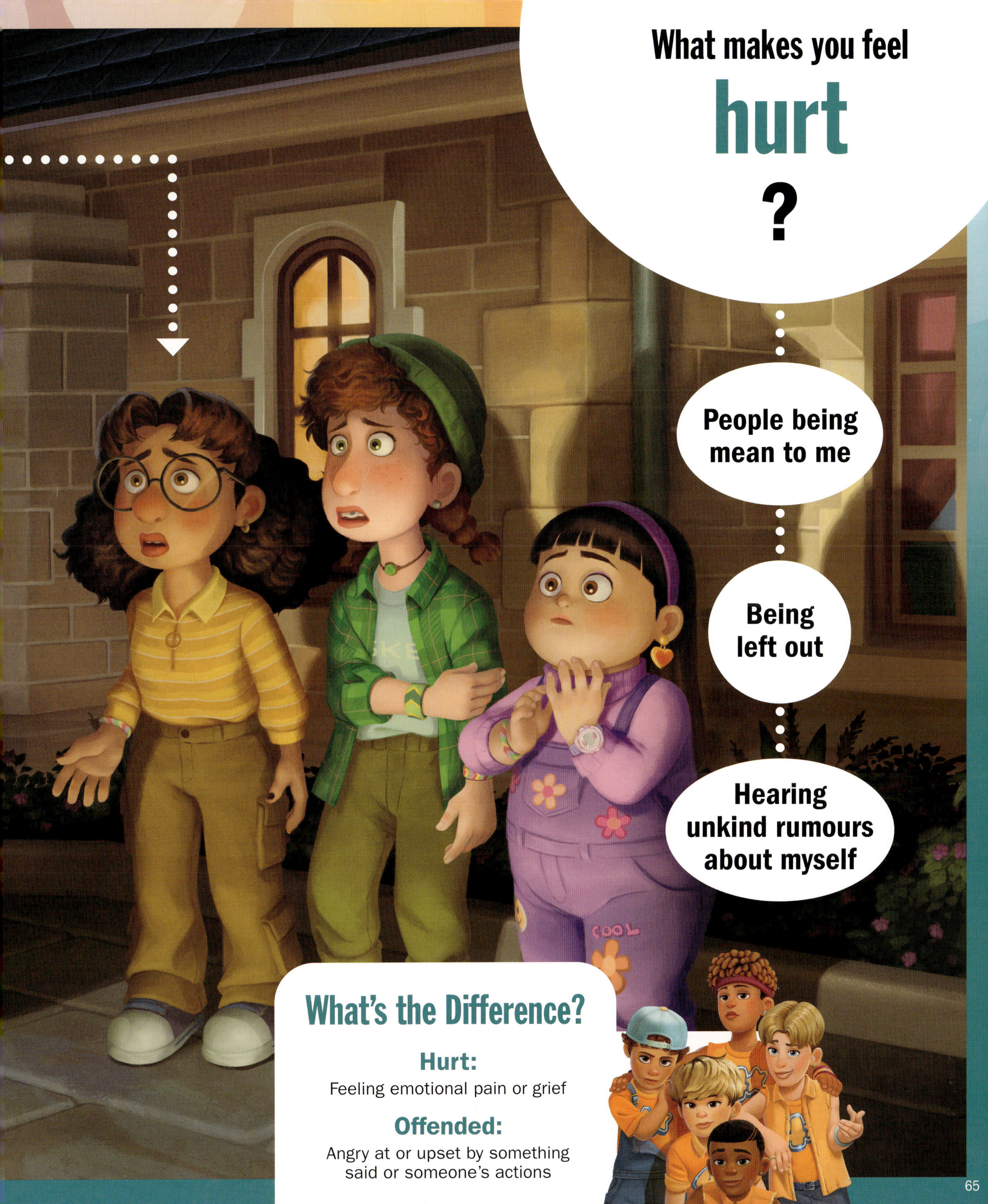

What's the Difference?

Hurt:
Feeling emotional pain or grief

Offended:
Angry at or upset by something said or someone's actions

Impatient

Accompanied by Zazu, Simba and Nala went to the water hole. Zazu remarked that Simba's parents would be thrilled the cubs were so friendly with each other. He explained there was an old tradition that dictated Simba would one day marry Nala.

Simba quickly became very **grumpy.** 'I can't marry her!' he scoffed. 'When I'm king, that will be the first thing to go. You'll have to do what I tell you.'

Simba thought that when he became king, he could act however he wanted to. 'I can't wait to be king!' he stated, **impatient.**

Talking About It

Simba was impatient and could not wait to become king. Have you ever wanted something so badly that you couldn't wait any longer? What did you do?

What are other times that you have felt impatient waiting for something to happen? What are some things we can do while we wait?

What makes you feel
impatient
?
Waiting for something I want
Thinking no-one is paying attention to me
Not getting my way
What's the Difference?
Impatient:
Irritated at having to wait
Grumpy:
Bad-tempered; irritable

Jealous

Snow White's wicked stepmother, the Queen, feared that someday Snow White's beauty would outshine her own. Each day, the Queen consulted her Magic Mirror. 'Magic Mirror on the wall, who is the fairest one of all?'

And each day the mirror replied, 'You are the fairest one of all.'

But one morning, the mirror declared that Snow White was the most beautiful woman in all the land, and the Queen flew into a **jealous** rage.

The **resentful** queen plotted against Snow White. She ordered her royal huntsman to take Snow White far into the forest and kill her.

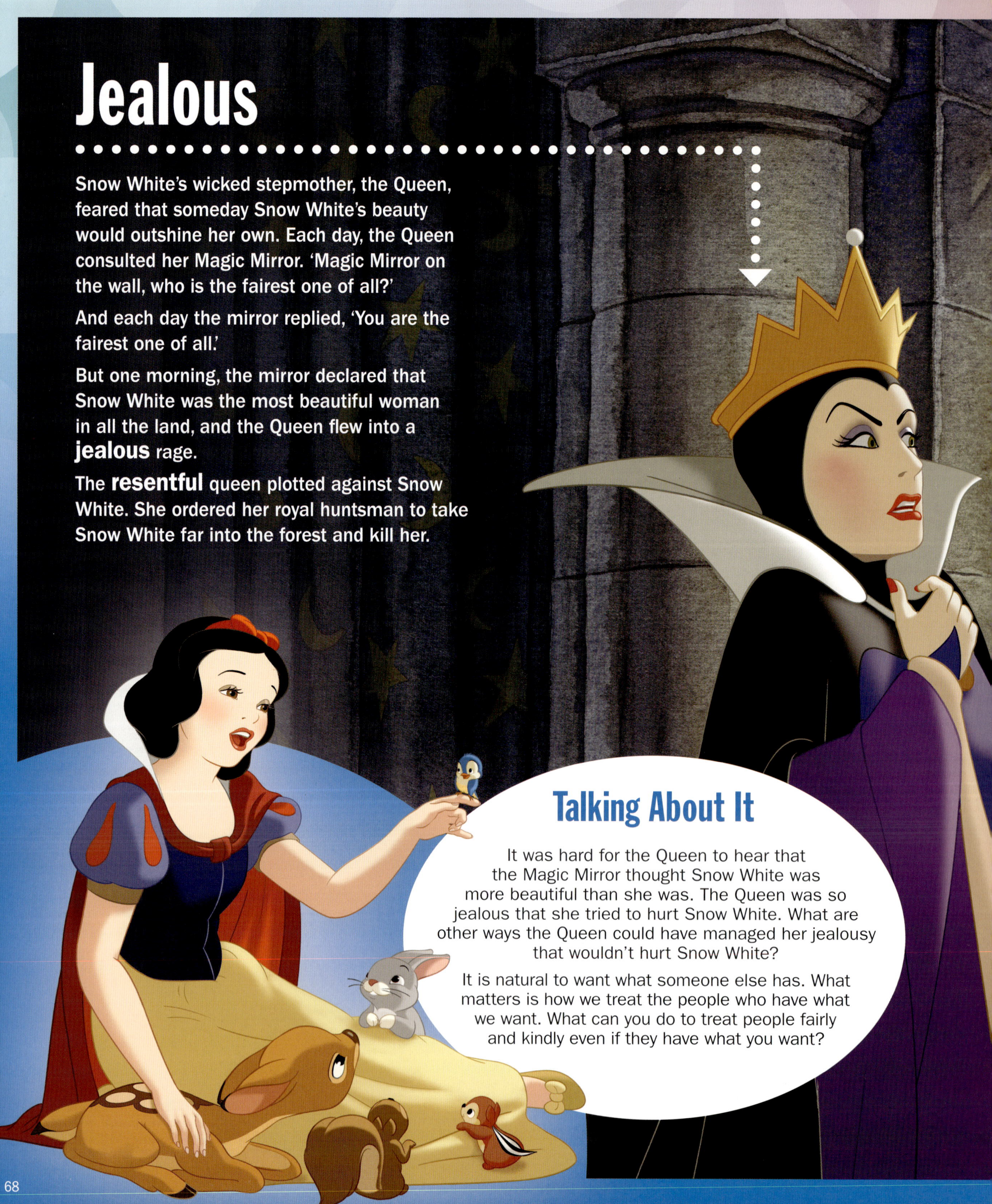

Talking About It

It was hard for the Queen to hear that the Magic Mirror thought Snow White was more beautiful than she was. The Queen was so jealous that she tried to hurt Snow White. What are other ways the Queen could have managed her jealousy that wouldn't hurt Snow White?

It is natural to want what someone else has. What matters is how we treat the people who have what we want. What can you do to treat people fairly and kindly even if they have what you want?

What makes you feel jealous?

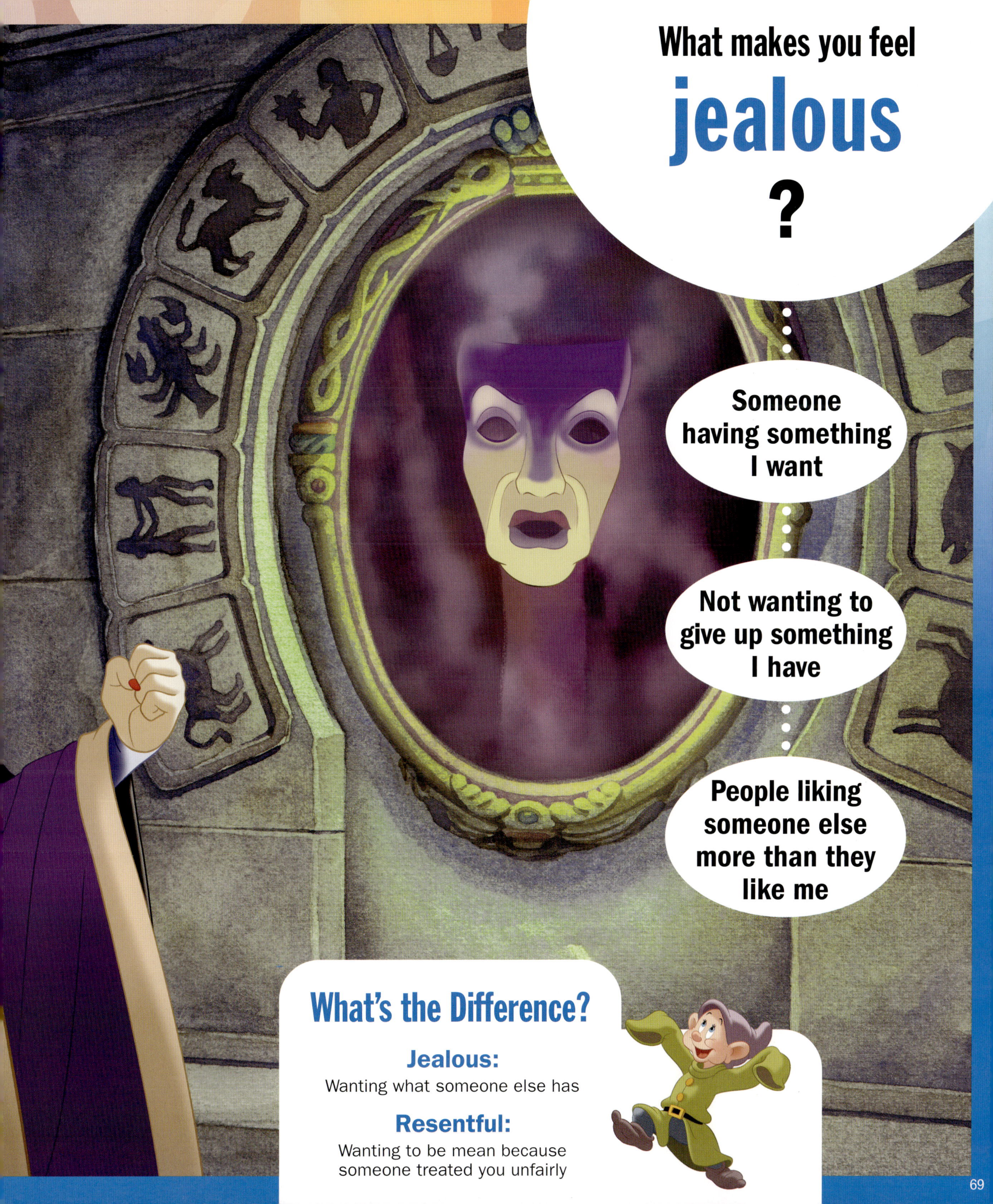

What's the Difference?

Jealous:
Wanting what someone else has

Resentful:
Wanting to be mean because someone treated you unfairly

Lonely

To help Stitch get settled for bed, Lilo read him a story, *The Ugly Duckling*. 'He's sad because he's all alone and nobody wants him,' Lilo explained. 'His family hears him crying, and they find him. Then the Ugly Duckling is happy because he knows where he belongs.'

This gave Stitch a lot to think about. Later, he went into the woods with Lilo's book and whispered, 'I'm lost.' Stitch felt **lonely** and **rejected** because he didn't know where he belonged.

Talking About It

Like Stitch, Lilo had a hard time fitting in. She felt lonely and wished for a friend. 'I need someone to be my friend, someone who won't run away,' Lilo said quietly.

Have you ever felt lonely in a new place? You may even feel lonely when surrounded by people. Why do you think you feel lonely when you aren't alone?

What makes you feel **lonely**?

Not being with my friends

Missing people I love

Not having anyone to play with

What's the Difference?

Lonely:
Feeling sad because you are alone

Rejected:
Not given approval or acceptance

Loved

The baby's ears were enormous! The lady elephants made fun of his ears. They made mean jokes about him and gave him a nickname: Dumbo.

Mrs. Jumbo was angry and whisked her baby away and held him close. She loved everything about him, especially his big ears. Dumbo smiled. His **caring** mother made him feel safe, warm and **loved.**

Talking About It

Dumbo's mum loved everything about him, even though others didn't understand some of the parts she loved. This made Dumbo feel supported and cared for.

Who in your life makes you feel supported or cared for? How do you feel when you think of these people?

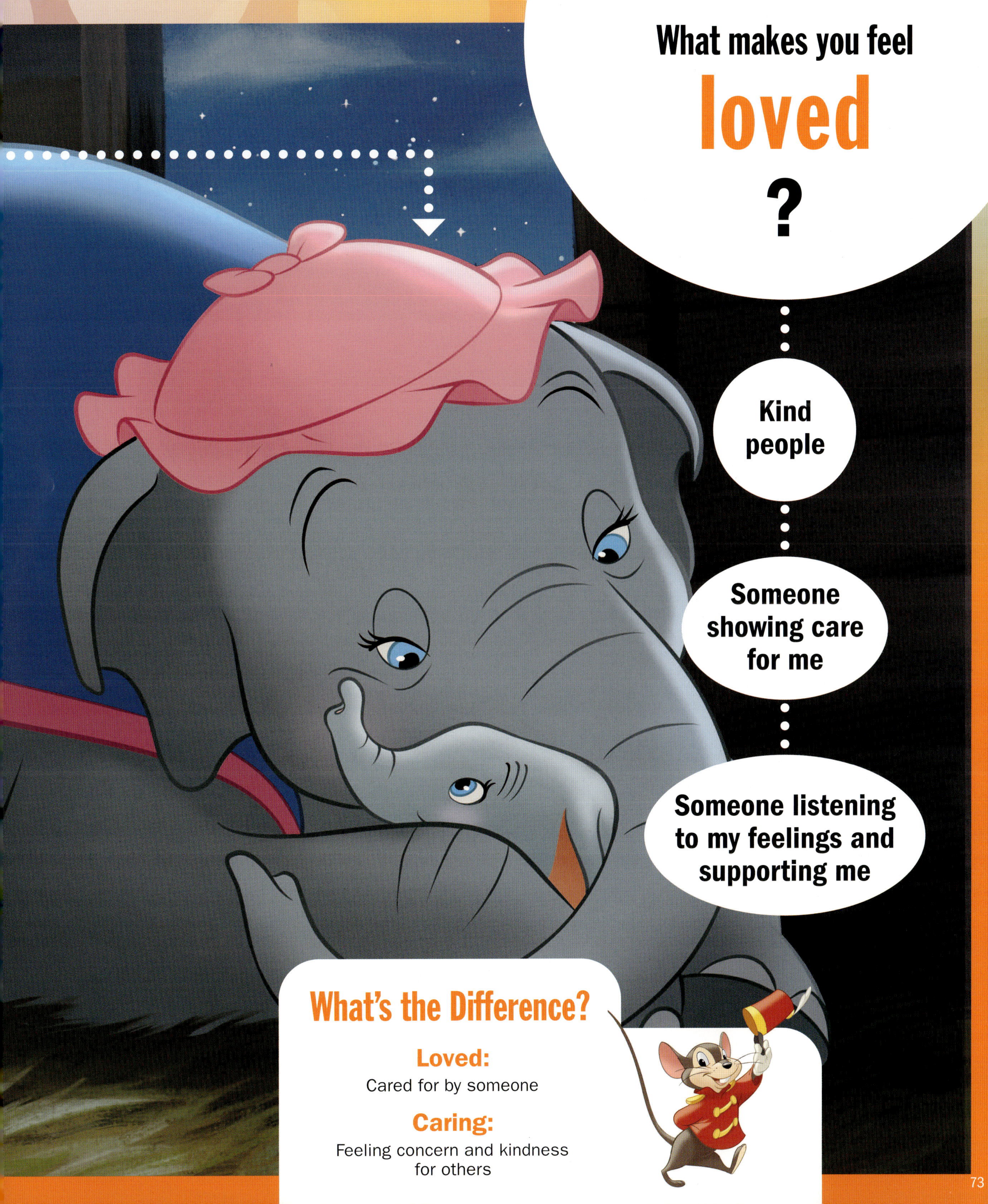
What makes you feel
loved
?
Kind people
Someone showing care for me
Someone listening to my feelings and supporting me
What's the Difference?
Loved:
Cared for by someone
Caring:
Feeling concern and kindness for others

Mad

Merida was a brave princess living in the Scottish Highlands. She loved exploring the forest despite the many dangers lurking in the shadows.

One evening, while the family enjoyed dinner together, Merida's mother made an announcement. Three neighbouring clans would each present a suitor to compete for Merida's hand in marriage.

Merida was shocked and **mad.** 'I won't go through with it!' she shouted before running out of the room. Merida was angry her future was being decided for her. **Fuming,** she rode away on her horse, Angus. Deep in the forest, Merida made a deal with a witch to gain control of her life.

Talking About It

Merida was mad at her mother for trying to decide her future. Merida wanted to choose her own path.

Has someone ever made it difficult for you to get what you wanted? Did you have mad feelings, like Merida? If you were Merida, how would you express your mad feelings in a healthy way?

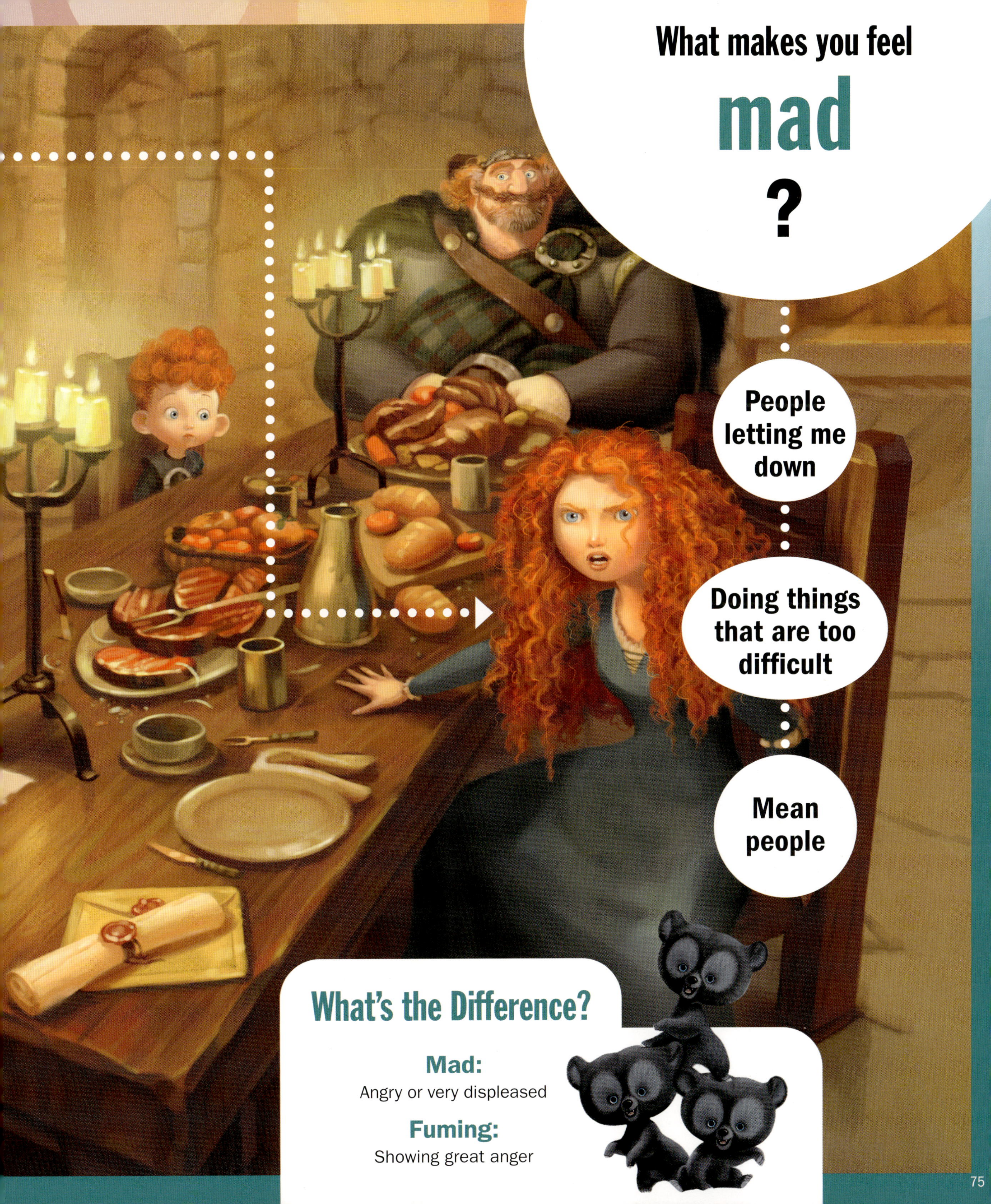
What makes you feel
mad
?
People letting me down
Doing things that are too difficult
Mean people
What's the Difference?
Mad:
Angry or very displeased
Fuming:
Showing great anger

Neglected

Poor Woody! Once Buzz arrived in Andy's room, nothing was the same. The cowboy posters on the wall were replaced with space posters. Andy stopped wearing his cowboy hat and started running through the house in a space costume.

Buzz was a hit with the other toys too. Everyone wanted to spend time with him. But the biggest shock was at bedtime. When Andy climbed under the covers, he took Buzz with him. Woody was left in the toy chest **ignored,** lonely, **neglected** and forgotten.

Talking About It

When Andy started to play more with Buzz than with him, Woody felt sad and neglected. Have there been times when you have been left out of playing with your friends? How did it feel? What did you do? When you see other people ignored or neglected, what can you do to be helpful to them?

When you feel ignored and neglected by people close to you, what can you do to let them know? How can you try to not neglect other people who may be feeling the same way?

What makes you feel **neglected** ?

People not paying attention to me

People not listening to me

Being left out by my friends and family

What's the Difference?

Neglected:
Not receiving enough attention; not cared for

Ignored:
Purposely unnoticed by others

Nervous

It was Antonio's big day, but he hid under a bed in the nursery. Mirabel found her little cousin and asked, 'Nervous?' Antonio sighed.

'You have nothing to worry about,' Mirabel said. 'You're going to get your gift and open that door and it's going to be the coolest ever.' Despite her reassurance, Antonio felt **nervous.** He was **afraid** something would go wrong at the ceremony.

It was time for Antonio to walk up the stairs towards his door. Mirabel held his hand to ease his nerves. As the two climbed each step, Mirabel remembered the day she didn't get her magical gift. Even though the memory made Mirabel more nervous for Antonio, she continued to help her cousin.

Talking About It

Antonio knew how important the ceremony was to his family and community. He worried it wouldn't work. Mirabel was there to comfort and support him, helping him feel less nervous.

When have you felt nervous? Who or what helped you through the situation?

What makes you feel **nervous** ?

Doing something I'm afraid of

Not knowing what will happen next

Being confused

What's the Difference?

Nervous:
Scared and easily alarmed

Afraid:
Fearful of something specific

Panicked

Ercole was searching for sea monsters offshore in his motorboat. Giulia was swimming, with Alberto and Luca rowing right behind her. Ercole spotted the trio, aimed his boat directly at them and gunned the motor.

'Oh, no!' gasped Giulia from the water. 'It's Ercole! Go, go!'

Alberto and Luca started to row furiously. But they were rowing in opposite directions, and the boat just spiralled.

'Why aren't we moving?' Luca gasped, **nervous,** out of breath and sweating.

Ercole's boat bore down on them. At the last minute, the boat swerved and sent up a huge wave that drenched Alberto.

Luca **panicked.** Alberto had transformed the second the water touched him. No-one could know their secret! Luca pushed Alberto overboard before anyone could see that he had changed into his sea monster form.

Talking About It

Feelings of being panicked usually come with feelings of being really scared. Luca was very scared that someone would see Alberto and find out their secret! How would you feel if you were Luca?

Luca panicked because he didn't know what others would think about Alberto and their secret. Have you ever felt panicked because you didn't know what would happen next? How did that make you feel?

What makes you feel panicked?

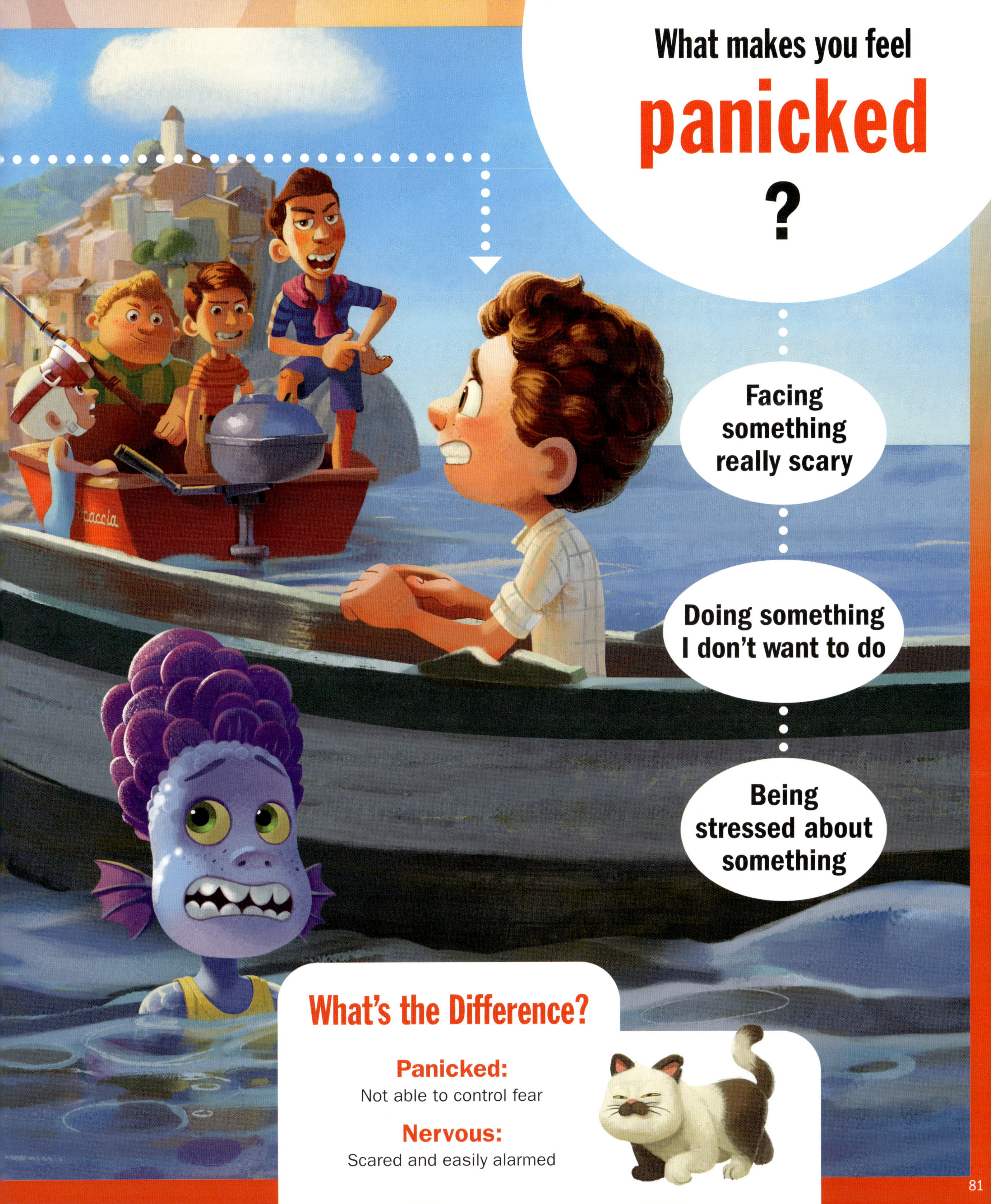

What's the Difference?

Panicked:
Not able to control fear

Nervous:
Scared and easily alarmed

Playful

Mei and her three best friends, Priya, Miriam and Abby, loved spending time together. Sometimes they would raise their voices and fight for causes they believed in. Sometimes they would hang out at school or fun parties.

Whenever Mei, Priya, Miriam and Abby were feeling **playful,** they would dance, sing and be **silly.** If their favourite song was playing, the girls would join in with loud singing and cool dance moves. It was easy for Mei to have fun with her best friends.

Talking About It

When Mei felt playful, she loved to sing and dance with her friends. What types of activities do you like to do when you feel playful? How does your body feel when you are in a playful mood? Are there certain people in your life who help you feel playful?

What makes you feel playful?

Having fun with friends

Participating in a silly activity

Using my imagination

What's the Difference?

Playful:
Feeling happy and having fun while doing something

Silly:
Funny and lighthearted

Proud

When Tiana was a little girl, she dreamt of opening her own restaurant. Her parents were supportive of her and encouraged Tiana to work towards her goal. As Tiana grew up, she never lost sight of her dream. She worked different jobs, perfected recipes and saved money.

It took years of determination and planning. After all her hard work, Tiana felt **proud** and **successful** when she opened her restaurant, Tiana's Palace. Just as she had imagined as a kid, she hosted friends, family members and the community. Tiana made her dream a reality.

Talking About It

Like Tiana, Louis had a dream. He loved jazz music and dreamt of playing with great musicians. Tiana helped by having Louis play at Tiana's Palace. At the restaurant, Louis played with a full jazz band!

Is there an activity or event you dream of doing? How would you feel if that dream came true? What is something you've done that has made you feel proud?

What makes you feel
proud
?
Finishing a difficult task
Doing well in an activity or a sport
Completing a goal
What's the Difference?
Proud:
Pleased with yourself or a personal accomplishment
Successful:
Having completed a goal or a plan

Sad

Ian Lightfoot never got to meet his dad. He had died before Ian was born. Ian learnt that his father was bold and wore purple socks. Ian decided to be bold, like his dad. Ian had dreams of speaking up more, taking driving lessons and inviting some kids to his birthday party, starting that day at school. However, the day didn't go as planned.

Back in his room, Ian felt like a failure. He felt **out of sorts,** because he didn't think he'd ever be bold and confident.

Ian clicked on a tape recording of his dad's voice.

He spoke in between his dad's sentences as though they were having a conversation. Ian was **sad.** He rested his chin on his hands and sighed. He wished more than anything that he could talk to his dad for real.

Talking About It

Ian felt sad that he would never get to meet his dad. Are there times when you are sad because you can't be with someone you care about? How do you feel at those times? What is something Ian could have done to feel less sad?

Have you ever lost something or someone you loved and felt sad that you wouldn't see that thing or person again? Were there other people or things that helped you feel better? What were they and what did they do?

What makes you feel sad?

Not being with people I care about

Losing something I love

Missing someone

What's the Difference?

Sad:
Unhappy and sorrowful

Out of sorts:
Not yourself; in low spirits

Scared

Ariel loved exploring the sea for human treasures. Her timid friend Flounder would often join her on these treasure hunts. One day, Ariel found a sunken ship to explore. As she sorted and picked through human tools and silverware, Flounder glanced around nervously. He heard something strange, and he was **scared.**

Chomp! A huge shark bit right through the ship. It began chasing Ariel and Flounder. They were **terrified** the shark would catch them. With some quick thinking and teamwork, Ariel and Flounder managed to get away. It took Flounder some time to settle his nerves after that adventure!

Talking About It

There are lots of things that can frighten us. Ariel and Flounder were scared of the big shark. Sebastian felt scared when he got caught by a chef who loved cooking seafood.

When have you felt scared? What did you do to feel less afraid? Are there certain places or things that make you feel scared? What can you do to manage these fearful feelings?

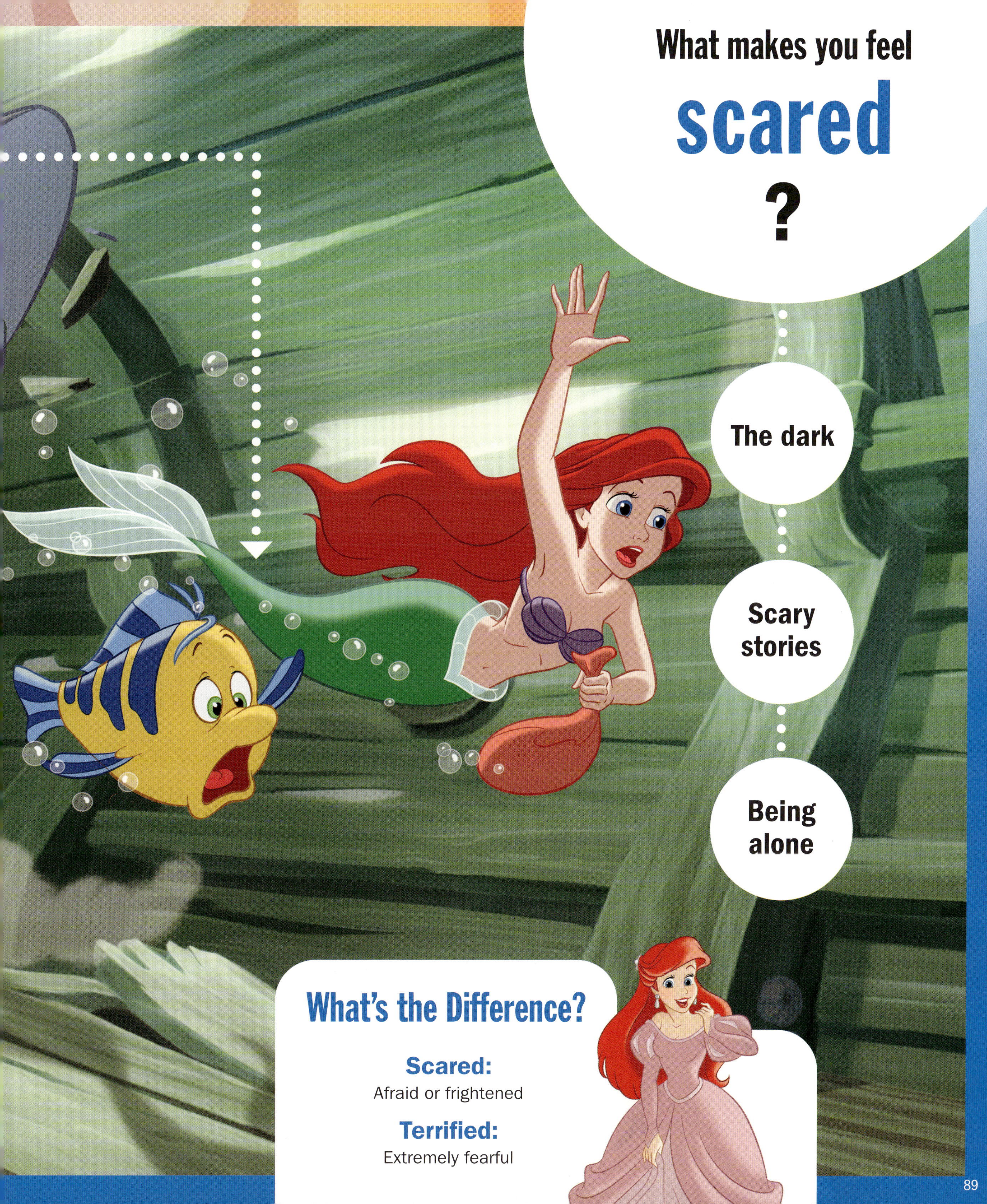

What's the Difference?

Scared:
Afraid or frightened

Terrified:
Extremely fearful

Shy

Baloo and Bagheera took Mowgli to the Man-village. Mowgli climbed a tree to get a good look at a beautiful girl he heard singing by the watering hole. Mowgli couldn't take his eyes off her. When the girl saw Mowgli, she smiled shyly at him. Mowgli suddenly grew **shy** and felt **timid** and scared and happy all at the same time.

Mowgli bravely climbed down from the tree and approached the girl. She dropped her jug, and it rolled to Mowgli's feet. He picked it up and followed the girl to the Man-village.

Talking About It

Everyone feels shy sometimes. Both Mowgli and the girl felt shy around each other when they first met. New people and new situations can be scary and can make us nervous about talking to others. When have you felt shy? What did you do?

It can help to have someone you trust with you in new situations or when meeting new people. Who are some people you trust to help you through new situations? Who are some people you could help in new situations?

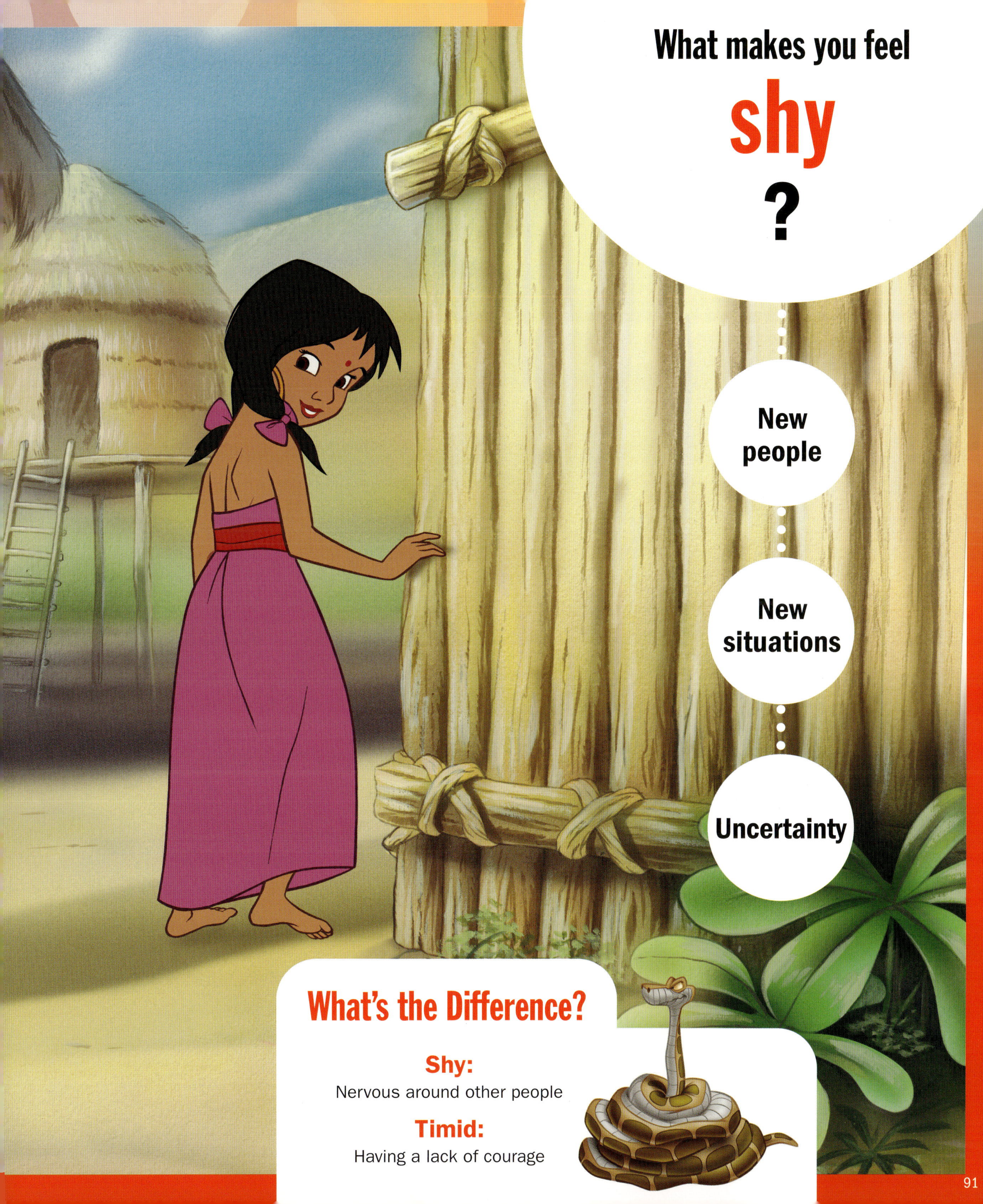

What makes you feel shy?

New people

New situations

Uncertainty

What's the Difference?

Shy:
Nervous around other people

Timid:
Having a lack of courage

Sorry

When Anna and Elsa were young, they played all sorts of imaginative games together. Using her ice powers, Elsa could create slides and snowmen for the sisters to play with. One night, while they were playing after bedtime, Elsa accidentally struck Anna with her ice powers. Their parents rushed into the room to see what had happened.

'It was an accident,' Elsa said. 'I'm **sorry,** Anna.' The family hurried to see the trolls, who were able to help heal Anna. But Elsa still felt **guilty** for hurting her sister.

Talking About It

The childhood accident affected Elsa and Anna's relationship as they grew up. Both sisters felt sorry for the distance that had grown between them. It took honesty, courage and love to heal their bond.

Have you ever felt like you upset someone? How did you feel? When you have been sorry, what helped you through the feeling?

What makes you feel sorry?

Knowing I made a mistake

Someone being disappointed in me

Doing something that hurts someone's feelings

What's the Difference?

Sorry:
Regretful for something you did

Guilty:
Feeling responsible for something that went wrong

Stressed

Everyone thought Linguini was a marvellous chef, capable of creating amazing sauces and soups. But Linguini had a secret. He was not a chef at all. His rat friend, Remy, was. Remy hid underneath Linguini's hat and guided Linguini while he cooked.

Keeping this secret made Linguini feel **stressed.** Not wanting to pretend anymore, Linguini prepared to tell the restaurant staff the truth. Remy stepped out and settled on Linguini's hand.

'A rat!' someone yelled.

Everyone in the kitchen grabbed something to hurl at Remy!

'Don't touch him!' shouted Linguini, feeling **worried.** Then he confessed at last that the little chef was the secret behind his success.

Talking About It

Linguini felt stressed because he had to hide Remy from the kitchen staff. He was constantly worried that someone would discover his secret.

Do you remember a time when you were stressed? What caused this feeling? How did you respond to the situation?

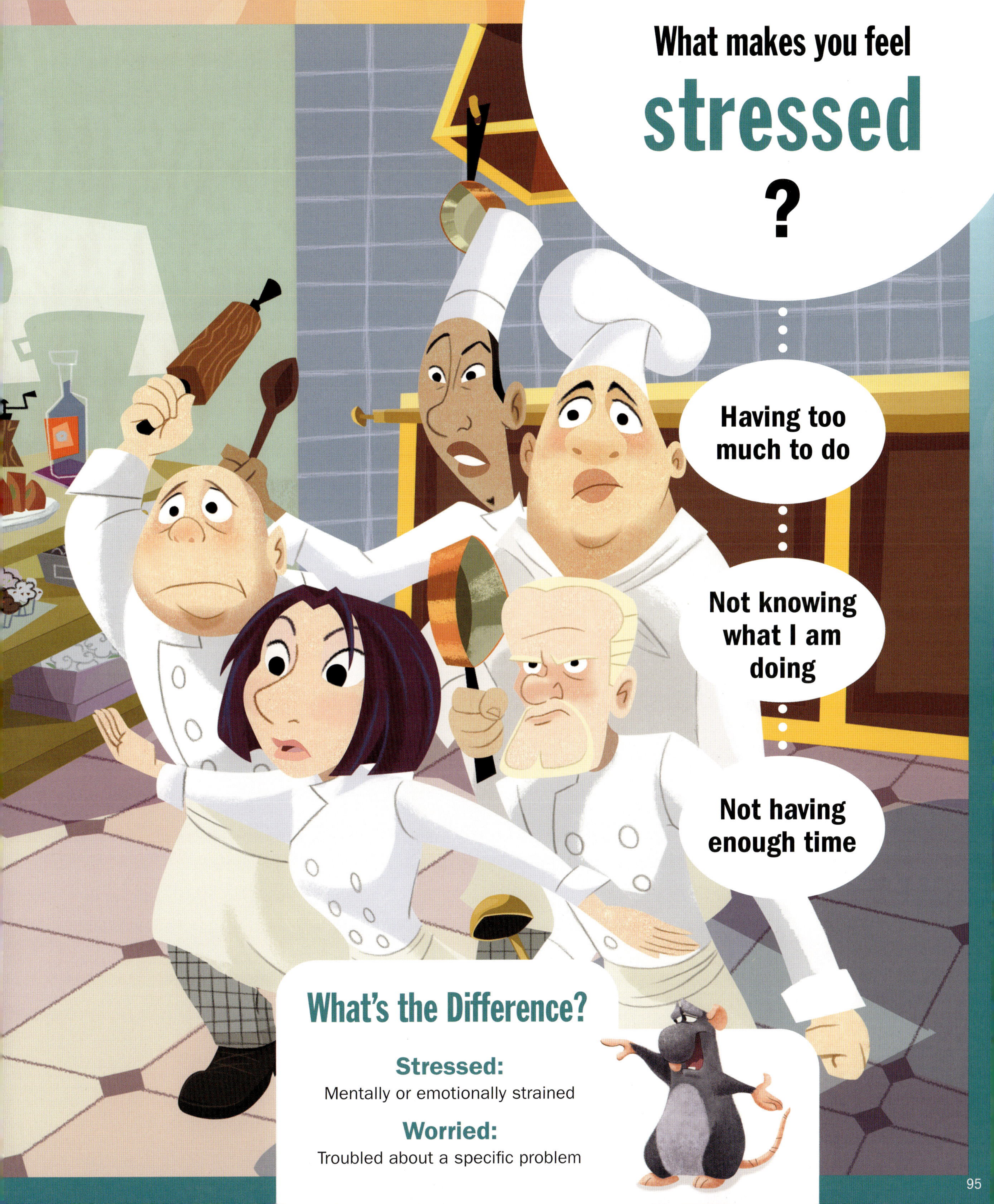
What makes you feel
stressed
?
Having too much to do
Not knowing what I am doing
Not having enough time
What's the Difference?
Stressed:
Mentally or emotionally strained
Worried:
Troubled about a specific problem

Surprised

When Asha was young, she and her father would climb a special tree, where they felt surrounded by stars. Her father said, 'The stars are there to guide us, to inspire us, to remind us to believe in possibility.' Years later, Asha sang to the sky from the very same tree. Suddenly, a bright ball of light shot down from the clouds.

At first, Asha had no idea what the quick, glowing orb was. It bounced through the forest, darting from flowers to trees to animals. When the ball of light finally slowed down, Asha was **surprised** and **excited** to see a magical star.

Talking About It

When Valentino met Star in the forest, it sprinkled stardust over his head. The little goat opened his mouth, and he could speak! He was surprised to have such a low voice.

When have you been surprised? Have you ever surprised someone the way Star surprised Asha and Valentino?

What makes you feel
surprised
?
Something unexpected happening
A surprise party
An exciting change in plans
What's the Difference?
Surprised:
Shocked by something unexpected
Excited:
Feeling eager happiness

Thankful

When Ember was little, her parents opened a shop called The Fireplace. Over the years, the family worked hard to run the shop. They were proud that it became the centre of the Fire community in Element City. Ember knew the shop was her dad's dream and tried her best to help it thrive.

But a citywide flood threatened the family dream. Floodwaters crashed into the shop, ruining everything inside. All seemed lost for The Fireplace. Luckily, the community came together to help. Ember was **thankful** for the many people who cleaned and rebuilt the shop. The community was **pleased** that The Fireplace reopened. The shop was busier than ever, enjoyed by people from all over Element City.

Talking About It

When different people from Element City helped Ember and her family, she felt thankful.

Has there been a time when you felt thankful for something others have done for you? Have you ever done something that made others feel thankful?

What makes you feel **thankful** ?

People being kind and helpful

Receiving something I want

Someone spending time with me

What's the Difference?

Thankful:
Grateful for someone or something

Pleased:
Happy or satisfied with a situation

Tired

Moana and Maui were on a quest to return the heart of Te Fiti. Their journey was filled with danger. The duo barely escaped Tamatoa, and Maui struggled to regain his full powers. When they faced Te Kā, the lava monster cracked Maui's hook. After these setbacks, returning the heart of Te Fiti seemed impossible. Moana pleaded with Maui to fix his hook and continue the quest.

'It was made by the gods!' Maui said. 'You can't fix it. Without my hook, I'm nothing!'

Maui was **tired.** The challenges on their journey had **exhausted** him. Maui transformed into a hawk and flew away. He didn't return to help Moana until he had rested his mind and body.

Talking About It

Maui was exhausted from facing so many challenges and setbacks. Have you ever worked really hard and been tired afterwards? How did you feel?

Sometimes when people are tired, they get impatient with other people. When you are tired, do you treat people differently? What is something you can do to avoid treating people badly when you are tired?

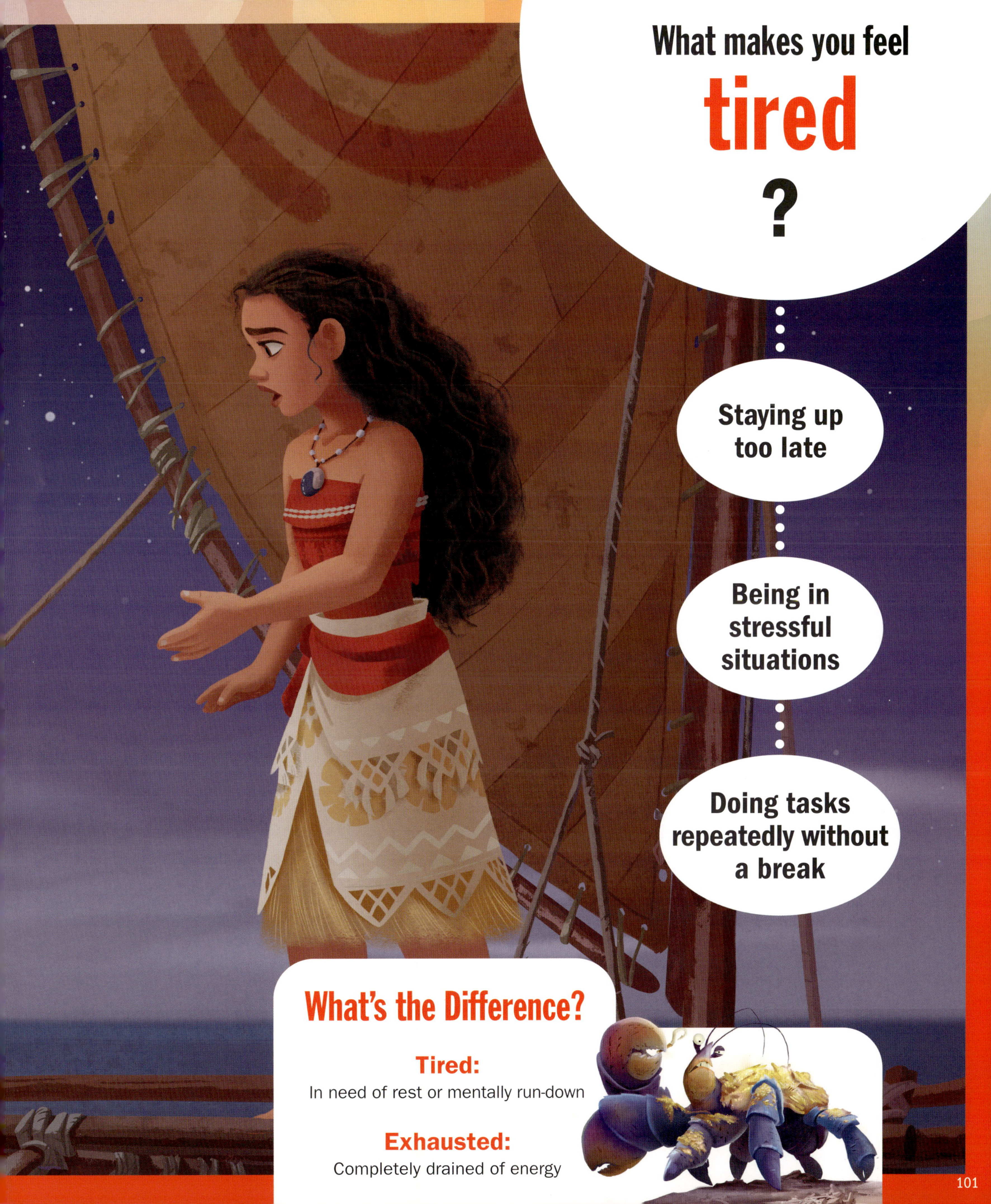

What makes you feel tired?

Staying up too late

Being in stressful situations

Doing tasks repeatedly without a break

What's the Difference?

Tired:
In need of rest or mentally run-down

Exhausted:
Completely drained of energy

Uncomfortable

The alien Experiment 626 escaped exile in space and crash-landed on Earth. He was being pursued by other aliens, who wanted to capture him and take him back to outer space. He was caught by Animal Control and taken to a shelter.

Nani and Lilo were at the same shelter the next day. Nani thought a puppy might keep Lilo company.

Experiment 626 made all the animals in the shelter **uncomfortable** and **irritated.** They were hiding from him. He knew Lilo was his only chance, because he was being chased by the other aliens and he didn't want to get caught. So he transformed himself to look more like a dog. Then he ran up to Lilo and threw his arms around her.

Lilo named him Stitch.

Talking About It

Stitch—or Experiment 626—acted differently from all the other animals in the shelter, and that made them uncomfortable. Have you ever felt uncomfortable because of how someone was acting or talking?

Not everyone will talk or act the same way we talk and act. When you are uncomfortable with something because it is different, how can you manage those feelings? Is there someone you can talk to about what you are feeling? What would you say?

What makes you feel
uncomfortable
?
Not being sure what will happen next
Something new
Someone talking about or doing something I don't like
What's the Difference?
Uncomfortable:
Uneasy
Irritated:
Slightly angry or annoyed

Upset

Wreck-It Ralph was visiting different video games in search of a winner's medal. He landed in Sugar Rush, a candy go-kart racing game. This was where he met Vanellope, a little girl who dreamt of racing. The two agreed to work together, making a go-kart for Vanellope to race. Vanellope promised to give Ralph the medal when she won.

But King Candy warned Ralph that Vanellope was a glitch in the game. If she raced, her glitching could get Sugar Rush unplugged. Ralph didn't know what to do. He felt **troubled.** To protect Vanellope, Ralph decided to wreck her go-kart. Vanellope was **upset** and hurt that Ralph would destroy her chance at racing.

Talking About It

Vanellope and Ralph faced upsetting situations in Sugar Rush. Even Fix-It Felix, who could usually fix anything, struggled when King Candy put him in jail.

Sometimes events or situations can make you feel upset. Think of a time when you were in a situation that made you feel upset. How did you respond? What can you do if you are dealing with something upsetting?

What makes you feel
upset
?
Things not going my way
Losing
Someone treating me badly
What's the Difference?
Upset:
Unhappy or disappointed
Troubled:
Having a problem

Worried

At hockey camp, Riley put a lot of pressure on herself. Her best friends would be going to a different high school, and Riley didn't want to be all alone. The only way to make sure that didn't happen was to get on the Fire Hawks team. To do that, she had to impress Coach Roberts. But Riley felt **worried.** Had she done enough to prove she belonged on the team?

Riley decided that reading Coach's notebook would help her figure out how to make the team. She snuck into Coach's office, **terrified** she would get caught. She knew what she was doing was wrong, but she was desperate to become a Fire Hawk!

Talking About It

Riley's worries about high school and becoming a Fire Hawk led her to some bad decisions. Have your worries ever made you think or act differently than you usually do? What helped you manage the situation in a healthy way?

Sometimes we are worried and don't know why. Have you ever felt this way? What helped you feel less worried?

What makes you feel
worried
?
Not knowing what will happen
Being confused about something
Scary thoughts
What's the Difference?
Worried:
Troubled about a specific problem
Terrified:
Extremely fearful

Explore Your Feelings

Understanding and expressing our feelings can be tricky. But we can practise ways to process and show the variety of emotions we all experience. Here are a few activities that can help you explore your own feelings.

Draw Your Feelings

Asha has a journal where she draws favourite moments and happy memories. Choose an emotion you have felt recently and draw a picture or silly cartoon to express it. When you look at your drawing, how do you feel?

Breathe Through Your Feelings

Mei learnt how to take calming breaths to process her feelings. Practising deep breathing can help you find your own calm. Sit comfortably, close your eyes and take slow breaths. How do you feel as you breathe slowly and deeply?

Shake Out Your Feelings

Ian, Barley and their dad dance it out together. Sometimes walking, stretching or dancing can help you identify and process your emotions. The next time you experience big emotions, try shaking out your feelings with some silly moves.

Act Out Your Feelings

Olaf is great at playing charades because he can rearrange his body! But you don't have to rearrange your body to act out emotions. Act out different emotions in front of a mirror or for friends and family to guess. How many different feelings can you act out?

Share Your Feelings

The members of the Parr family often share their feelings with each other. Practise identifying how you feel and sharing those thoughts with a trusted friend or adult. Learning how to share your emotions can make it easier to find your calm when you have big feelings.

Glossary

adventurous: daring, not afraid to take risks
afraid: fearful of something specific
aggravated: angered or displeased by small problems
agitated: disturbed and upset
alarmed: feeling shock or sensing danger
amazed: filled with wonder by something or someone
annoyed: a little angry or irritated
anxious: worried about something specific
ashamed: deeply regretful about something you did

B

bitter: feeling hurt or upset for a long time
bored: having no interest in what you are doing
bothered: concerned about something
brave: having courage; ready to face something dangerous, scary or difficult

C

calm: quiet and peaceful
caring: feeling concern and kindness for others
comforted: feeling calm and supported
confident: believing in oneself
confused: not understanding, or feeling lost
content: satisfied; peaceful and happy
curious: excited to learn about or know something

D

disappointed: sad because something didn't happen the way you hoped
discouraged: losing confidence or excitement
disgusted: strongly disapproving
dismayed: troubled or upset
distracted: having trouble focusing or concentrating

E

eager: really wanting to do something
elated: really happy
embarrassed: feeling stress about how others see you
enthusiastic: interested in and excited about something
excited: feeling eager happiness
exhausted: completely drained of energy

F

friendly: kind and interested in other people
frustrated: bothered that things aren't going your way
fuming: showing great anger
furious: full of anger; very mad

G

grumpy: in a bad mood
guilty: feeling responsible for something that went wrong

H

happy: pleased and content
hateful: filled with hatred
helpful: willing to give assistance or support to others
hopeful: feeling that something might turn out well in the future
hurt: feeling emotional pain or grief

I

ignored: purposely unnoticed by others
impatient: irritated at having to wait
indifferent: having no interest
irritated: slightly angry or annoyed

J

jealous: wanting what someone else has

L

lonely: feeling sad because you are alone
loved: cared for by someone

M

mad: angry or very displeased
moody: having sudden changes in mood, sometimes getting sad

N

neglected: not receiving enough attention; not cared for
nervous: scared and easily alarmed

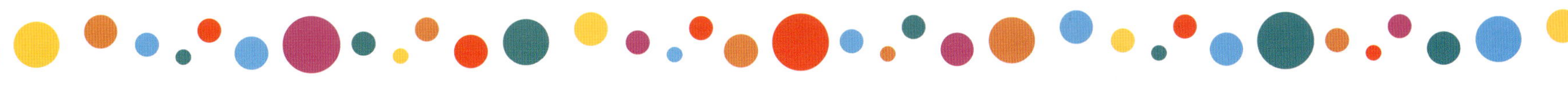

O

offended: angry at or upset by something said or someone's actions
out of sorts: not yourself; in low spirits
outgoing: confident around other people

P

panicked: not able to control fear
playful: feeling happy and having fun while doing something
pleased: happy or satisfied with a situation
positive: upbeat and hopeful
proud: pleased with yourself or a personal accomplishment

Q

questioning: wondering and showing an interest in learning about something

R

rejected: not given approval or acceptance
relaxed: being at rest and having a sense of ease
resentful: wanting to be mean because someone treated you unfairly
restless: unable to relax

S

sad: unhappy and sorrowful
scared: afraid or frightened
shy: nervous around other people
silly: funny and lighthearted
sorry: regretful for something you did
stressed: mentally or emotionally strained
successful: having completed a goal or a plan
surprised: shocked by something unexpected

T

terrified: extremely fearful
thankful: grateful for someone or something
thrilled: very pleased with a situation
timid: having a lack of courage
tired: in need of rest or mentally run-down
troubled: having a problem

U

uncomfortable: uneasy
unhappy: sad; not happy
unpleasant: disagreeable; filled with unhappiness
upset: unhappy or disappointed

V

vengeful: wanting to get back at someone out of anger

W

worried: troubled about a specific problem

Index